Pirates on the High Seas

The United States and Global Intellectual Property Rights

Bénédicte Callan

From the Study Group on American
Intellectual Property Rights Policy

Bénédicte Callan, Project Director
Ellen L. Frost, Chair

Council on Foreign Relations, Inc., a nonprofit, nonpartisan
nal membership organization founded in 1921, is dedicated to
oting understanding of international affairs through the free
ivil exchange of ideas. The Council's members are dedicated
belief that America's peace and prosperity are firmly linked
t of the world. From this flows the mission of the Council: to
America's understanding of its fellow members of the international community, near and far, their peoples, cultures, histories,
hopes, quarrels and ambitions; and thus to serve, protect, and ad-
vance America's own global interests through study and debate,
private and public.

**THE COUNCIL TAKES NO INSTITUTIONAL POSITION
ON POLICY ISSUES AND HAS NO AFFILIATION WITH
THE U.S. GOVERNMENT. ALL STATEMENTS OF FACT
AND EXPRESSIONS OF OPINION CONTAINED IN ALL
ITS PUBLICATIONS ARE THE SOLE RESPONSIBILITY
OF THE AUTHOR OR AUTHORS.**

For further information about the Counil or this Paper, please
contact the Public Affairs Office, Council on Foreign Relations,
58 East 68th Street, New York, NY 10021.

CONTENTS

ACKNOWLEDGMENTS

THIS PAPER WAS inspired by the presentations and discussions of the Council on Foreign Relations study group American IPR Policy after the TRIPs Agreement: The Current and Future Agenda. I am greatly indebted to its members for many of the insights and ideas presented here, and to Ellen Frost, the chairwoman of the study group, for her ability to keep discussion crisp and pertinent. The study group taught me much about intellectual property rights and American trade policy, but while our discussions provided fodder for thought, the ideas presented here are not the product of a consensus reached by study group participants and should not be attributed to anyone other than me.

Albert Fishlow has been utterly invaluable for his thoughtful comments on multiple drafts of this paper. Ann Markusen, Gregory Noble, and Miles Kahler helped identify key problems and issues. The sharp editing of Dooley Adcroft and Sean Costigan's tireless revisions have tightened the writing. My thanks also go to the Council's excellent library staff—Leigh Gusts, Connie Stagnaro, and Marcia Sprules in particular—who gathered invaluable information for me on this topic. Finally, I thank Peter Fitzpatrick for his help in organizing the study group, and Harpreet Mann and Nomi Colton-Max for their enthusiastic research assistance.

FOREWORD

AMONG THE MOST notable accomplishments of the new World Trade Organization is the Trade-Related Intellectual Property Rights Agreement, which brought the issue of intellectual property rights into a multilateral trade framework for the first time. A nation's intellectual property policy had previously been a domestic issue, loosely coordinated through the World Intellectual Property Organization. With the inclusion of intellectual property rights in the Uruguay Round agreement, differences between countries became a legitimate subject of trade disputes. The Council on Foreign Relations assembled a Study Group, chaired by Ellen Frost of the Institute for International Economics, to assess the effects of the TRIPs agreement and consider potential U.S. policies to combat the piracy of intellectual property around the world.

In this paper, Bénédicte Callan argues that a change in strategy on intellectual property is necessary, not so much because American goals have changed as because the challenges are new. Japanese and European ambivalence, Asian reluctance, and enforcement problems all present obstacles to further progress if the United States continues to pursue a bilateral strategy. Regional agreements such as the North American Free Trade Agreement and the Asia-Pacific Economic Cooperation might play an important role in the coordination of national intellectual property policies and the creation of global standards, but they cannot be superimposed willy-nilly onto the global system. Instead, the United States should infuse intellectual property rights in future multilateral forums while considering three new tactics: (1) pursuing standards for big emerging markets separate from other developing countries; (2) providing aid to those developing countries that attempt to enforce intellectual property rights; and (3) opening an internal debate on the place of intellectual property in overall U.S. trade policy.

As technology becomes a greater part of trade and trade itself becomes a bigger proportion of economic activity, U.S. interests in global intellectual property rights have become a critical aspect of trade policy. New information technologies and bioscience-based treatments will make international agreements on intellectual property rights more urgent. The United States needs a coordinated strategy, with a long-term objective of creating a sustainable discussion on intellectual property standards with developing countries. Trade conflicts cannot be avoided, but battles should be carefully chosen to ensure that the U.S. position occupies the high ground. Callan puts forth the case that a new strategy requires the United States to deemphasize bilateralism and pursue more active regional and multilateral strategies.

Gary C. Hufbauer
Director of Studies
Council on Foreign Relations
December 1997

MEMBERS OF THE STUDY GROUP

Chair
ELLEN L. FROST, Senior Fellow, Institute for International
    Economics

Project Director
BÉNÉDICTE CALLAN, Fellow, Council on Foreign Relations

Participants and Speakers
SARAH ALEXANDER, The World Bank
ROBERT ANTHOINE, Winthrop, Stimson, Putnam & Roberts
HARVEY BALE, Pharmaceutical Research and Manufacturers
    of America
JUDITH H. BELLO, Sidley & Austen
BETSY BIEMANN, The International AIDS Vaccine Initiative
CARLOS ALBERTO PRIMO BRAGA, The World Bank
DANIEL F. BURTON, Novell, Inc.
SARAH C. CAREY, Steptoe & Johnson
ROBERT B. CHARLES, Subcommittee on National Security
ISABELLA CHUNG, U.S. Council for International Business
STEVEN C. CLEMONS, Office of Senator Jeff Bingaman
HORACE G. DAWSON, Jr., Howard University
EDWIN DEAGLE, Systems Research and Applications, Inc.
JOHN DIEBOLD, The JD Consulting Group
WILLIAM ELLIS, IBM
G. A. PETER FITZPATRICK, Council on Foreign Relations
ISAIAH FRANK, Johns Hopkins University
FRANCINE FRANKEL, University of Pennsylvania
HARRY FREEMAN, The Freeman Company
JOSEPH GAVIN, U.S. Council for International Business

RONNIE LEE GOLDBERG, U.S. Council for International Business
JACQUES J. GORLIN, The Gorlin Group
CARL J. GREEN, Asian Law and Policy Studies
JOSEPH A. GREENWALD, Consultants International Group
KOICHI HAMADA, Yale University
MARTHA CALDWELL HARRIS, Department of State
WILLIAM HASELTINE, Human Genome Sciences
MICHAEL HODIN, Pfizer
GARY HUFBAUER, Institute for International Economics
MERIT JANOW, Columbia University
KENNETH H. KELLER, Council on Foreign Relations
PETER KENEN, Princeton University
DAVID LATHAM, Lovell, White & Durrant
DEBORAH LEHR, Office of the U.S. Trade Representative
ROBERT J. LEMPERT, RAND Corporation
RACHEL LEVINSON, OSTP
CHUCK LUDLAM, Biotechnology Industry Organization
MANJULA M. LUTHRIA, Georgetown University
COLM MACKERNAN, Global Technology Management
JOHN MAGGS, Journal of Commerce
DIANE MARKOWITZ, Department of State
ANN MARKUSEN, Council on Foreign Relations
KEITH MASKUS, University of Colorado
ROBERT MORRIS, U.S. Council for International Business
EMILY MOTO MURASE, Federal Communications Commission
KATE H. MURASHIGE, Morrison & Foerster
M. ISHAQ NADIRI, New York University
WALTER O'CONNOR, Fordham University
J. THOMAS RATCHFORD, George Mason University
BONNIE RICHARDSON, Motion Picture Association
DAVID SCHMICKEL, Biotechnology Industry Organization
ROBERT SHERWOOD, International Business Counselor
MICHAEL SOLTON, Steptoe & Johnson
RICHARD STERN, Ablondi and Foster

Members of the Study Group

FREDERICK S. TIPSON, AT&T
MARK TRAPHAGEN, Software Publishers Association
CHARLES WEISS, JR., Global Technology Management
JOHN WILSON, Information Technologies Industry Council
MICHAEL K. YOUNG, Columbia University
PETER ZIMMERMAN, Independent Consultant

I have no doubt that if I could poll American readers, or American Senators . . . or even American booksellers, that an assent to an international copyright would be the result. The state of things as it is is crushing to American authors, as the publishers will not pay them on a liberal scale, knowing that they can supply their customers with modern English literature without paying for it . . . It is equally injurious to American booksellers—except to two or three of the greatest houses. No small man can now acquire the exclusive right of printing and selling an English book. If such a one attempt it, the work is reprinted instantly by one of the leviathans—who alone are the gainers. The argument of course is that American readers are the gainers—that as they can get for nothing the use of certain property they would be cutting their own throats were they to pass a law debarring themselves from the power of such appropriation. In this argument all idea of honesty is thrown to the winds . . . The ordinary American purchaser is not much affected by slight variations in price. He is at any rate too high-hearted to be affected by the prospect of such variation. It is the man who wants to make money, not he who may be called upon to spend it, who controls such matters as this in the United States.

—Anthony Trollope, 1876

INTRODUCTION

THE AMERICA THAT Anthony Trollope came to know as an English emissary in the 1870s is entirely unfamiliar to contemporary readers. Despite their nominal protection in the U.S. Constitution, Trollope encountered indifference and resistance from American officials in his efforts to enforce copyrights for literary works.[1] His eloquent arguments about the benefits of strong intellectual property protection for the domestic literary market fell on deaf ears. Yet a century later, an older and more prosperous United States casts itself as the great proponent of intellectual property rights worldwide. Modern American negotiators take the moral high ground in the battle against international piracy and counterfeiting, denouncing unfair practices abroad and claiming that stronger rights can only help the economy in developing countries. Much has changed in a hundred years.

The switch in the U.S. position is understandable. A country's level of development heavily influences the value placed on intellectual property rights. Developing countries have always been leery of strong IP protection, which favors innovators over consumers, creative production over diffusion, and private interests over social goals. In Trollope's time, the United States was just becoming an international economy and remained unconvinced that IPR enforcement was a necessity. The U.S. position changed with its status in the world. In fact, just a few years after Trollope's visit, the United States came to see the value in international intellectual property cooperation, and joined Europe in signing the Paris Convention for the Protection of Industrial Prop-

---

[1] The U.S. Constitution lays out the intention "To promote the Progress of Science and useful Arts, by securing for limited Times to Authors and Inventors the exclusive Right to their respective Writings and Discoveries," Article 1, section 8.

[1]

erty (1883) and the Berne Convention for the Protection of Literary and Artistic Works (1886). An era of international cooperation opened, and while IPRs were mainly of domestic concern, countries extended national treatment to foreign firms. Decades of relative quietude passed, during which intellectual property remained an arcane and technical field populated by inventors and lawyers.

In the 1980s intellectual property suddenly became the cause célèbre of trade politics, and the United States quickly became a formidable proponent of global IP rights. The United States has had showdowns with half a dozen countries over their IP policies. Twice, altercations with the People's Republic of China have brought the United States to the brink of a trade war. The Trade-Related Intellectual Property (TRIPs) Agreement is in many respects the heart of the new World Trade Organization (WTO). The United States concocted a policy of aggressive unilateral pressure for key countries with weak IP regimes to curb their piracy rates and maintain American incentives to innovate despite a world of porous international boundaries. Through the use of the Special 301 clause in the 1988 Trade Act, the General Agreement on Tariffs and Trade (GATT) negotiations on TRIPs, and the North American Free Trade Agreement (NAFTA), the United States brought intellectual property to trade's center stage. The policy was a radical break with the past, and it coincided with a change in America's position in the world economy.

This activist IP policy was formulated amid the economic and security upheavals of the 1980s, which included the globalization of business, the yawning trade deficit, slow growth rates, and Asian competition. Its first objective was to strengthen American exports in the entertainment and technology industries—the so-called information industries of the future. If the United States could recapture $25 billion of sales lost to piracy, a very optimistic scenario, exports would rise by about five percent.[2] The second objective of the policy was to combat the free rider problem inherent in industrial research and development (R&D) investments. When piracy is rampant, industrial R&D essentially becomes a nonexcludable and nonrival good (i.e., companies at home and abroad are loath to invest in research since its fruits are easily available to all for free).[3] Reinforcing research incentives for U.S. firms should encourage them to maintain technological leadership. A third and related objective was to expand the innovation pie for all countries. Enhancing the appropriability of knowledge in developing countries should not only help local innovators but also facilitate technology transfers, trade in technology goods, and foreign direct investment. Increasing access to technology should spur growth in developing countries, and growing export markets are good for U.S. business.

In an era of such economic turmoil, an aggressive global intellectual property policy was perceived as necessary to champion American jobs, exports, and growth. The idea was not to coddle weak industries. In fact, the industries in the IP limelight—software, entertainment, and pharmaceuticals—were already stars of the American economy; big, dynamic sectors that exported their products worldwide. For example, in the 1980s the personal computer created a mass market for business software estimated at $8 billion, and jobs for software engineers boomed, growing by 156 per cent over the decade.[4] Looking more broadly at informa-

---

[2] According to the International Monetary Fund, total U.S. exports in 1994 were $465 billion; see *1994 International Financial Statistics Yearbook*.

[3] Nonexcludable means that a company cannot prevent others from using its ideas or products. Nonrival means that one person's use of the good does not detract from another's enjoyment of it. When a good is nonexcludable and nonrival, the private sector has a tendency to underinvest in its production.

[4] By comparison, the growth rate in jobs nationwide was a modest 12% over the same period, according to the U.S. Bureau of the Census' *Statistical Abstract of the United States: 1995*.

tion industries, almost five percent of the U.S. work force is employed, directly or indirectly, in copyright-dependent sectors—including software, music, film, and print.[5] The vitality and promise of these industries are embodied in their growth rates, which have recently been twice as high as that of the U.S. GDP (5.6 per cent versus 2.7 percent between 1991 and 1993)[6] Worldwide revenues from video entertainment—films, TV, and rentals—grew by 16 percent in 1993, and video games alone have become an impressive $12 billion industry with a 40 percent annual growth rate.[7]

In addition to their contribution to growth rates and employment, the intellectual property-dependent industries are important because they export. Copyright industries exported $45.8 billion in 1993, second only to the automotive industry. Chemical products, which include pharmaceuticals and other goods heavily reliant on patent protection, exported $45.1 billion that year.[8] In general, "high-technology" goods are increasingly important to trade, accounting in the United States for more than 52 percent of all merchandise trade and growing 17 percent faster than trade in all goods from 1985 to 1993.[9]

---

[5] Just under six million people, or 4.8% of the U.S. work force, work in copyright-related areas; see National Intellectual Property Association, "Copyright Industries in the U.S. Economy: 1977–1993," Washington, D.C., 1995.

[6] International Intellectual Property Association (IIPA), "Copyright Industries in the U.S. Economy: 1977–1993," Washington, D.C., 1995.

[7] For total revenues of $23.7 billion; see IIPA, "Copyright Industries in the U.S. Economy: 1977–1993." The growth rates are for 1987–93 as quoted in Gary Nelson, "The Sufficiency of Copyright Protection in the Video Electronic Entertainment Industry: Comparing the U.S. with the European Union," *Law and Policy in International Business,* vol. 27, no. 3 (1996), p. 805.

[8] IIPA, "Copyright Industries in the U.S. Economy: 1977–1993."

[9] Maskus, "Regionalism and the Protection of IPRs," unpublished paper presented to the Council on Foreign Relations study group American IPR Policy after the TRIPs Agreement, April 19, 1996.

Introduction

Piracy is, therefore, a scourge because it affects the symbols of American industrial strength—modern information-intensive industries—in which the United States places its greatest hopes for the future. Remember also that this IP strategy was forged in the dying embers of the Cold War, just as the United States was getting its first glimpses of a liberal trade regime on an unprecedented geographic scale. At stake, therefore, is not simply the competitiveness of a handful of U.S. industries but the shape of the entire international R&D system—who pays for innovation, and who benefits from it. Developing countries see American policy as an attempt to freeze the present technological division of labor, and not entirely unreasonably, they accuse the United States of technological protectionism.[10] The United States emphasizes the incentives for creativity that stronger IPRs promise for all countries.

Despite skepticism abroad, from 1986 to 1996 American powers of persuasion worked to improve the level of international IP protection. Dozens of bilateral agreements have raised protection levels in the four corners of the globe. The GATT TRIPs Agreement was signed, NAFTA included an intellectual property agreement, and the Asia-Pacific Economic Cooperation (APEC) forum is considering doing so. Anthony Trollope would hardly recognize this new world. Yet the success of American IP policy has bred its own problems, and U.S. policymakers are struggling with how to proceed in further raising IP standards abroad. The second term of the Clinton administration offers the opportunity to redefine intellectual property policy, to clarify its goals and make it more consistent across countries.

The following article explores the types of strategies open to the United States in its effort to continue combating global piracy in a

---

[10] For this argument see Paulo R. de Almeida, "The Political Economy of Intellectual Property Protection: Technological Protectionism and the Transfer of Revenue among Nations," *International Journal of Technology Management*, vol. 10, no. 2/3 (1995), pp. 214–29.

post-TRIPs environment. A change in strategy is necessary, not because American IP goals have changed but because the challenges are different. First, the momentum of the Uruguay Round has dissipated, leaving the United States with little visible support from Japan and Europe in its efforts to raise IP standards globally. Second, bilateral negotiations will produce fewer results, both because the United States has already concluded the easy bilateral IP agreements and because the tools it once relied upon to force changes abroad have become blunt with wear. [11] Third, no matter what means are used, extracting further IP concessions in the developing world is going to become more difficult and expensive, especially as the U.S. must now contend with typical behind-the-border monitoring and enforcement problems. Finally, the countries the United States most wants to reach are in Asia. They are neither as vulnerable to U.S. demands as Latin America was, nor as interested in a rule-based trade agreement.

If the United States is committed to furthering the harmonization of IP systems internationally, it has three policy options—a deepening of multilateral commitments through the World Trade Organization, the forging of regional agreements with an intellectual property dimension, or the country-by-country negotiation of bilateral IP agreements within the parameters allowed by the WTO. The present administration, much like its predecessors, has a predilection for bilateral negotiations. This paper argues that, while effective for a limited number of countries, in order to build a global IP system, the U.S. emphasis should be on putting IPRs front and center in future multilateral forums.

---

[11] Harvey Bale suggests that for a number of reasons the American strategy of using sticks to encourage the enactment of stronger IPRs has reached an impasse. See Harvey Bale, Jr., "External Pressure: Does It Work? The Case of Pharmaceuticals," unpublished paper for the Council on Foreign Relations study group American IPR Policy after the TRIPs Agreement, Washington, D.C., June 6, 1996.

Introduction

Asia, as the home to some of the most inveterate IP infringers, will be the proving ground for American policy in the near future. At the moment, neither APEC nor the WTO seems capable of convincing recalcitrant Asian countries to upgrade their IP regimes. The United States will be tempted to rely on bilateral agreements to raise standards in specific nations. But a bilateral strategy is too expensive and inconsistent to employ on a large scale. And while regional agreements have an important role to play in coordinating national IP policies and creating global standards, regional strategies cannot fully achieve U.S. goals either. Neither strategy should be pursued to the detriment of broader multilateral agreements that will bring all countries into a single system and provide a predictability attractive to the developing countries that sign on.

This paper starts by briefly reviewing the recent history of U.S. IP policy (Section 2); what global IP standards have been achieved (Section 3); and why the United States, given its present IP strategy, must expect iterative rounds of negotiations before satisfactory levels of international protection are achieved. Next the challenges to American IP policy are described, including the growing price tag and geographic spread of piracy (Sections 4); and the difficulty of eradicating piracy because of its behind-the-border character (Section 5). The U.S. government must choose among possible strategies and goals for combating global piracy (Section 6); and its choices are constrained by important political and financial considerations (Section 7). Finally, Section 8 uses Asia as an example of the comparative effectiveness of regional and multilateral agreements in raising IP standards.

THE EVOLUTION OF
U.S. IP POLICY

IN THE 1980S AMERICAN intellectual property policy evolved from ad hoc to a coordinated policy of forcing change in trading partners whose standards were considered below par. The acts committed by IP infringers were really no more egregious than in the past, but U.S. interests and conditions in the world changed to make them unacceptable, and the world changed, allowing America to take action. Over the course of the 1980s, the United States redefined lax global IPRs as a threat to its economic strength, and created a multitrack strategy to combat piracy at multiple levels.

Americans began to treat international IP disputes with the gravity reserved for unfair trade practices once they became conscious of the dangers inherent in economic globalization for U.S. competitiveness. Americans have since become accustomed to hearing about the "global economy" and thinking that the United States has a privileged but precarious position as an economic superpower. But in the early to mid-1980s, Americans were very anxious about four macroeconomic problems: new international trade patterns, U.S. balance of payment problems, an overvalued dollar, and slow growth rates. Deep fears about the ability of the U.S. economy to compete led many in government to believe that liberal economic policies were hampering U.S. firms. Open U.S. markets were thought to be a mistake if foreign markets were less open or trade policies not symmetrical. The 1980s, therefore, gave birth to a protectionist backlash. Selective reciprocity—the belief that liberalization should only be offered on a tit-for-tat basis—

came to characterize much of U.S. trade policy, including that on intellectual property. [12]

The most disturbing macroeconomic trend was the skyrocketing deficit in the balance of payments, which reached well over $100 billion per year in the mid-1980s, due mostly to a surge in imports of manufactured goods, particularly automobiles and parts, industrial supplies and materials, and consumer goods. [13] In addition, the United States became acutely aware during this period that it no longer reigned unchallenged as global economic leader. U.S. trade as a percentage of world trade was dropping, during a period in which the importance of international trade was growing. The decline was natural, as Japan and Europe had recovered rapidly after the war, but the emergence of newly industrializing countries like Taiwan and Korea as strong exporters was worrisome, and the United States became much more sensitive to the perceived "unfair trade" practices of its partners.

In addition, the United States found itself slipping in some key high-technology sectors. [14] In industries like semiconductors, microelectronics, and machine tools, the rapid loss of world market share sparked a debate about the future of American growth and competitiveness and exacerbated tensions in trade relations with Asia. [15] High-technology trade had become very important to the United States: recent figures show that in the advanced industrial-

---

[12] One of the classic texts exploring the economics of selective reciprocity as a trade strategy is Paul Krugman, ed., *Strategic Trade Policy and the New International Economics*, Cambridge, MA: MIT Press, 1986.

[13] See U.S. Department of Commerce, *U.S. Foreign Trade Highlights;* Washington, D.C., 1995, pp. 11–15.

[14] For a history of high technologies in the U.S.; see Richard R. Nelson and Gavin Wright, "The Rise and Fall of American Technological Leadership: The Postwar Era in Historical Perspective," *Journal of Economic Literature,* vol. 30 (December 1992), pp. 1,931–64.

[15] For a review of high technology trade disputes, see Laura D'Andrea Tyson, *Who's Bashing Whom?* Washington, D.C.: Institute for International Economics, 1992.

ized countries, over half of total trade flows are in high-technology sectors.[16] Furthermore, the growth of high-technology trade is faster than the total rate of growth for all trade. Losing market share in such large and growing export sectors was cause for concern. Technology-intensive products and entertainment were an island of export strength in an era of poor American economic performance, and they were directly threatened by weak intellectual property rights abroad. Since intellectual property is an important component of most high-technology products, American firms lobbied to raise the level of protection afforded abroad.

By the end of the 1980s, not only did the United States have strong motivations to protect American intellectual property on a global scale, but for the first time in half a century, it was also at liberty to do so. *Glasnost* and *perestroika*—the elements of Soviet liberalism that ultimately led to the end of the Cold War—freed American economic diplomacy from the shadow of grand security concerns. It was no longer necessary to overlook the economic peccadilloes of U.S. trade partners for the sake of a stronger military alliance. Trade consequently moved up the ladder of U.S. national priorities. In addition, American timing was fortuitous. The early 1980s were a period of deep economic turmoil marked by oil and banking crises that hobbled many developing countries.[17] In response, countries chose to adopt more liberal economic policies to escape the crisis. From 1985 to 1995, foreign direct investment in a range of developing countires rose from between 100 percent and tenfold.[18] While the investments provided capital and technol-

---

[16] Maskus, "Regionalism and the Protection of IPRs."

[17] This point is made by Susan Sell, "Intellectual Property Protection and Antitrust in the Developing World," *International Organization*, vol. 49, no. 2 (Spring 1995), pp. 315–49.

[18] See Carlos M. Correa, "Intellectual Property Rights and Foreign Direct Investment," *International Journal of Technology Management,* vol. 10, no. 2/3 (1995), pp. 173–99.

ogy, they also made governments—especially in Latin America—more vulnerable to American IP demands. The coincidence of American activism with such important shifts in the international economic order made power IP politics possible.

The United States Trade Representative (USTR) under the Reagan administration first articulated a "multitrack" approach to trade. The idea was to expand multilateral discussions, while continuing to engage countries in bilateral agreements and intensifying unilateral pressures.[19] In intellectual property this entailed an American shift away from the World Intellectual Property Organization (WIPO)—responsible for oversight of the major international intellectual property conventions—where discussions of IPR harmonization had stalled due to WIPO's single-issue focus and proclivity to weigh developing nation concerns heavily.[20] Instead, the USTR, at the prodding of American industries, pushed a novel IP initiative onto the agenda of the GATT Uruguay Round. The United States continued to engage in bilateral discussions, especially with Japan, but as the largest importer in the world, it also decided to toughen its unilateral IP demands.

Most emblematic of the new IP vigilance was the Trade and Competitiveness Act of 1988. The amended Section 301 requires the USTR to investigate countries that "have a history of violating existing laws and agreements dealing with intellectual property rights." [21] Countries whose observance of intellectual property rights are subpar are put on a "watch" list, which opens bilateral

---

[19] For further discussion of the multitrack policy, see Sylvia Ostry, *Governments and Corporations in a Shrinking World,* New York: Council on Foreign Relations, 1990, pp. 25–30.

[20] WIPO was created in 1967. It administers the Berne Convention, the Rome Convention, the Geneva Convention, and the Paris Convention. Organizationally, WIPO's one-nation, one-vote organization favors the less-developed countries, which are more numerous.

[21] Definition from I.M Destler, "American Trade Politics," Washington, D.C.: Institute for International Economics, 1995, p. 318

discussions. The worst offenders—called priority foreign countries—can be subject to retaliatory sanctions if bilateral discussions do not lead to a change in practices. Much to the chagrin of other nations, Section 301 has been a powerful stick for shaping foreign IP practices, especially those that rely heavily on exports to the American market. Of the countries named "priority foreign countries," only Brazil did not act to change IP practices to the U.S. government's satisfaction, resulting in the imposition of trade sanctions.[22] (See Table 1 for a listing of all priority foreign country cites and investigations under Section 302(b)(1) of the Trade Act.)

Countries have changed their behavior to avert sanctions or simply to avoid being cited on the watch list by the USTR. The United States also linked intellectual property to the Generalized System of Preferences (GSP) and other benefits for developing countries ranging from International Development Bank loans to the funding of joint scientific projects.[23] These "sticks," combined with the persistent prodding of state and private delegations, forced the issue of stronger IP protection on U.S. trade partners.

In the mid-1990s, the United States continues to press hard for intellectual property protection despite the fact that the economic outlook is arguably much rosier, at least from a U.S. perspective. Domestically, the United States enjoys a "dream economy" of low inflation, low unemployment, reasonable growth, and a growing stock market. Internationally through 1996, the dollar had become more competitive, the current account deficit was improving (as a percentage of GDP), and exports were growing at a brisk

---

[22] In 1987 Brazil was named priority foreign country for its lack of pharmaceutical patents. Retaliatory tariffs affecting $39 million Brazilian exports per year remained in place for two years. For a general discussion of the success of the use of Section 301, see Alan O. Sykes, "Constructive Unilateral Threats in International Commercial Relations: The Limited Case for Section 301," *Law and Policy in International Business,* vol. 23, no. 2 (1992), pp. 263–331.

[23] The Generalized System of Preferences is a set of preferential market access measures for developing countries. The Caribbean Basin Initiative and the Andean Trade Preferences Act also linked to intellectual property protection.

Table 1. Section 301 and 302 Intellectual Property Investigations

		Resolution
Argentina	1988	agreed to better pharmaceutical patent protection, case withdrawn
Brazil	1985	on informatics policy and related IP protection, case withdrawn
	1987	sanctions imposed because of lack of pharmaceutical IP protection, sanctions lifted when product and process protection agreed to, 1990
	1993	agreed to enact a new patent law, case withdrawn
Chile	1988	pharmaceutical patent complaint withdrawn by initiating party
China	1991	agreed to improve general IP protection, case withdrawn
	1994	memorandum of understanding signed, case withdrawn
	1996	negotiated enforcement, case withdrawn
India	1991	for general intellectual property protection, case remains open
	1996	WTO Dispute Settlement (DS) Panel on pharmaceutical and agrichemical patents, case remains open
Pakistan	1996	WTO DS Panel on pharmaceutical and agrichemical patents, reached agreement
Portugal	1996	request WTO DS on TRIPs patent term, reached agreement
S. Korea	1985	agreement reached on stronger IP protection
	1987	pharmaceutical patent complaint withdrawn by initiating party
	1988	two pharmaceutical patent complaints withdrawn by initiating parties
Taiwan	1992	agreement reached on stronger IP protection, monitoring compliance
Thailand	1990	agreed to amend and enforce copyright laws, monitoring compliance
	1991	inadequate pharmaceutical patent protection, U.S. delaying action
Turkey	1996	WTO DS Panel, box office tax, case open

Source: USTR Website—http://www.ustr.gov.

rate. [24] Still, defensive efforts continued to protect the most vibrant "knowledge-intensive" industries and to facilitate their ability to compete worldwide. Most of the impetus, however, comes from three main sectors: software, pharmaceuticals, and entertainment.[25] The argument put forward by these sectors is that without strong intellectual property protection abroad, the technology industries would have trouble recouping high development costs and would probably invest less in research. A slightly different logic applies for the print, music, and film industries. Since protection abroad is usually not necessary to guarantee domestic investment, U.S. support of copyright protection is a matter of propping up profits and stemming losses in one of the United States' strongest export sectors.[26] For better or worse, these industries continue to define international IP policy within the USTR, often without much domestic debate and in the absence of any larger trade policy context.[27]

---

[24] The United States has regained some self-confidence and optimism about economic prospects, now that the Europeans are mired in double-digit unemployment and the Japanese are just barely pulling themselves out of a four-year recession.

[25] While these industries continue to produce trade surpluses for the United States, the surplus in advanced technologies has been declining since 1991. See National Science Board, "Science and Engineering Indicators, 1996, " Washington, D.C.: National Science Foundation, 1996.

[26] The International Intellectual Property Alliance (IIPA) calculates that copyright-protected industries accounted for $238.6 billion in value added to the U.S. economy, or 3.74% of the gross domestic product. From 1991 to 1993 the industries grew at more than twice the rate of the U.S. economy, and employment growth in copyright industries grew four times the national employment growth rates between 1988 and 1993. Foreign sales grew 11.7% in 1993, to an estimated $45.8 billion, second only to sales of motor vehicles and parts. More than half is due to software sales, 18% to motion pictures, 16% to records and tapes, and 8% to print. See Jon Schaffer, "Copyright Protected Industries Outpacing Other U.S. Sectors," February 16, 1995. United States Information Agency website—http://www.usia.gov/topics/ip/ipr58.htm.

[27] When there is debate about the appropriate format of domestic IP protection, however, the debates are heated. Examples of issues still unresolved in the United

The U.S. commitment to raise world IP standards is thus designed to buttress the comparative advantage of American firms in a more global economy by all possible means. As long as American comparative advantage lies in knowledge-intensive products, processes, and designs, and as long as these are easily appropriated and disseminated abroad, the United States will have a significant stake in shaping the global management of intellectual property.

I would argue, however, that the mid-1990s are not the mid-1980s, and the United States does have a choice about whether it wants to continue its activist bilateral policies or adopt a more comprehensive, transparent, and equitable global IP policy. I believe the latter creates a more solid platform from which to build new multilateral agreements on intellectual property. Aggressive unilateralism has reached an impasse, which provides an opportunity to redefine the goals and methods of U.S. policy.

States include the patenting of genetic sequences and the breadth of copyright protection to be extended to on-line information and databases. In the latter, the U.S. Patent and Trade Office is pitted against the Library of Congress, the National Education Association, and the Internet service providers. See Denise Caruso, "Global Debate over Treaties on Copyright," *The New York Times*, December 16, 1996, p. D1.

THE TRIPs AGREEMENT
AND BEYOND

BILATERAL TOOLS HAVE been successful in raising IP standards abroad, but they are, in the long run, inefficient. They target one country at a time, work best only in the countries that are most dependent on access to U.S. markets, and result in a patchwork of agreements.[28] The GATT Uruguay Round negotiations, which opened in 1986, presented a golden opportunity to turn intellectual property rights into a multilateral trade issue. With the Trade-Related Intellectual Property Rights Agreement, the United States cast its net wider, in one swoop intensifying and harmonizing the IP regulations of all WTO countries.[29] The agreement was a fantastic success, achieving far more than its backers initially expected, but it has not ushered in an extended era of multilateralism for intellectual property. To the contrary, TRIPs has given the United States new tools with which to badger recalcitrant countries, especially in the developing world.

Among the less-developed countries (LDCs), the TRIPs accord was highly controversial. The LDCs initially opposed the uniform IP standards proposed in TRIPs, much preferring the World Intellectual Property Organization's position that countries should set standards according to their level of development—a solution unacceptable to the United States. India and Argentina, among others, argued that stronger rules would impose heavy costs and a

---

[28] Susan K. Sell, "Intellectual Property Protection and Antitrust in the Developing World."

[29] TRIPs was initially drafted through the efforts of the "Intellectual Property Rights Committee," a private group of U.S. industrialists called together by the USTR, and by two top industrial organizations in Europe and Japan, the Union of Industries of the European Community and Keidanren.

[16]

loss of control over technology diffusion. Over time, however, a reluctant consensus formed around TRIPs, aided by the unpopularity of U.S. unilateral pressure, the use of cross-issue bargaining, and changing attitudes in the South—especially Latin America— toward the benefits of trade and IP rights. Essentially, the developing world came to endorse TRIPs as the lesser of two evils. In exchange for binding minimum standards and a dispute-settlement mechanism, developing countries hoped TRIPs would rein in the aggressive unilateralism of American IP diplomacy.

The NAFTA Background

The North American Free Trade Agreement, completed two years before the conclusion of the GATT Uruguay Round, also helped the ratification of TRIPs enormously by raising the stakes.[30] Article 17 of NAFTA stipulated high and uniform standards of protection for Canada, Mexico, and the United States, setting the terms for TRIPs negotiations.

First, NAFTA established a long patent term and stated that inventions—product or process—in all fields should be patentable. (Exceptions were made for inventions that threaten public safety or morality, as well as for biotechnological, therapeutic, and surgical inventions.) The broad scope of patent protection benefits, most notably, the pharmaceutical and agrochemical industries, whose products were often excluded from patent protection in developing countries (including Italy and Japan up to the 1970s). Second, NAFTA extended copyright protection to new technologies such as encrypted satellite signals, software databases, and sound recordings. Third, NAFTA limited the conditions under

---

[30] Negotiations for the Uruguay Round opened in 1986. The TRIPs agreement was signed in Marrakesh in April 1994 and went into force January 1, 1996. The NAFTA agreement was signed in December 1992 and approved by the U.S. Congress in November 1993, and entered into force January 1994.

which compulsory licensing is permissible, strengthened the contractual rights in copyrights, and constrained parallel importation. Finally, NAFTA stipulated that the IP agreement would enter into force almost immediately and member countries would have to establish procedures expeditiously for the enforcement of property rights.

Because NAFTA could theoretically be broadened to include other Latin American countries, it set a standard for future trade liberalization. And therein lies its importance for the TRIPs Agreement. Because new entrants will have to have equivalent standards, NAFTA is credited with accelerating substantial changes in the Southern Cone's IP laws—notably in Chile, Brazil, and even Argentina.[31] Indeed, Latin American intellectual property regimes look more and more promising, with MERCOSUR and the Free Trade Association of the Americas (FTAA) seriously discussing IP standards.[32] And while data is still scarce, the experience of Mexico and other countries is beginning to confirm liberal economic theories that stronger intellectual property rights have positive effects on trade, investment, and domestic innovativeness.[33] The prospect of firmly anchoring the Southern Cone in a liberal trading system with a strong IP component is very real, and will be a boon for developers of intellectual property.

---

[31] See Carlos Alberto Primo Braga, "Chile and NAFTA: The Services and Intellectual Property Rights Dimensions," unpublished paper for the Chile NAFTA Seminar of the World Bank and the Ministry of Finance of Chile, Santiago, June 20, 1994.

[32] Robert M. Sherwood and Carlos A. Primo Braga, "Intellectual Property, Trade and Economic Development: A Road Map for FTAA Negotiations," unpublished paper, 1996.

[33] For articles on the trade and investment effects of stronger IPRs see Maskus, "Regionalism and the Protection of IPRs," and Edwin Mansfield, "Intellectual Property Protection, Foreign Direct Investment, and Technology Transfer," Discussion Paper 19, Washington, D.C.: International Finance Corporation, 1994. It is interesting to note, however, that the data on technology transfer remain inconclusive.

With major Latin American countries on board the IP band-wagon, developing countries elsewhere saw the writing on the wall. Stronger intellectual property rights have become a signal of commitment to economic liberalization and integration into the international trading system. Politicians and the public in many—though not all—developing countries now believe that stronger intellectual property rights can be an aid to development, and consequently their opposition to the TRIPs agreement has weakened.

TRIPs' Strengths

In April 1994 a truly new framework for global intellectual property rights emerged with the successful conclusion of the Uruguay Round. Like NAFTA, TRIPs established a minimum standard of protection for a broad range of intellectual property devices, including patents, copyright, trademarks, and trade secrets. [34] For the first time in history, all the disparate intellectual property types were brought under one pan-national convention. Furthermore, the minimum standards of protection demanded from the 120 WTO signatories broke an old tradition in which a diversity of IP systems was accepted as long as each country granted national treatment to foreigners. WTO members thus gave up a degree of freedom in setting domestic IP laws in exchange for greater international uniformity. A new twist was added to the national treatment clause: countries must also extend (in the majority of cases) most-favored-nation treatment for intellectual property rights, meaning that any advantage granted to one country has to be extended to all other WTO countries.

---

[34] Jacques J. Gorlin elaborates on the strengths and weaknesses of the TRIPs agreement in "U.S. Intellectual Property Policy after TRIPs," unpublished paper for the Council on Foreign Relations study group American IPR Policy after the TRIPs Agreement, June 1996.

A broad range of areas is covered in TRIPs. The highlights of the requirement for each type of protection follow[35]:

- Patents—granted for 20 years from the date of filing. Obligations based on the Paris Convention for the Protection of Industrial Property (1967). The only products or processes that are not necessarily eligible for patent protection are those that endanger the public order or morality; diagnostic, therapeutic, or surgical methods; (non-micro-biologic) plants and animals; and biological processes. "Pipeline" protection will temporarily be granted to pharmaceutical and agricultural products in countries that are allowed to delay implementing full patent protection.

- Copyrights—obligations based on the Berne Convention for the Protection of Literary and Artistic Works (1971) and the Rome Convention (1961). Computer programs, databases, sound recordings, movies, and performances are protected for 50 years. Broadcasts receive 20 years of protection. Rental rights—the right to authorize or prohibit commercial renting—is provided for software and sound recordings. Neighboring rights—protecting the performances of copyrighted works—are protected for performers, producers, and broadcasting companies. National treatment is not required for Rome Convention signatories.

- Trademarks—registered for 7 years initially, and can be renewed indefinitely. Governments may require that the trademark be used within the country. Prohibits the compulsory licensing of trademarks.

- Semiconductor Layouts—10-year protection for layout designs. Compulsory licensing is not allowed. Based on the

---

[35] Based in part on the description of the TRIPs agreement in Jeffrey Schott, *The Uruguay Round: An Assessment*, Washington, D.C.: Institute for International Economics, 1994, pp. 115–23 and 168–70.

Treaty on Intellectual Property in Respect of Integrated Circuits (1989).

- Geographic Indications—prohibits use of indications that can mislead consumers as to the true origin of the product. Further negotiations mandated for a multilateral system of registration and notification.

- Industrial Designs—10-year protection "against unauthorized making, selling, or importing copies of new or original industrial designs."[36]

- Trade Secrets—include internally derived documents or processes. Companies are granted protection from misappropriation and unauthorized use as long as they take reasonable steps to keep information private.

Thus the TRIPs agreement covers, though to a lesser degree than NAFTA, new fields and technologies. Semiconductor layouts are protected, and biotechnology-derived microorganisms and processes are patentable. Other genetically altered life forms, or parts thereof, are left to the discretion of the member countries. Plants must be included in the International Union for the Protection of New Varieties of Plants (UPOV) even if a country decides not to extend patent protection.[37] However, many information technologies—including information on the Internet and satellite signals—are left out of the TRIPs agreement entirely.

A major innovation not found in NAFTA is the establishment of a formal WTO enforcement and dispute-settlement mechanism to adjudicate complaints of member nations. In theory, countries

---

[36] Schott, "The Uruguay Round: An Assessment."

[37] The UPOV Convention provides a *sui generis* form of protection for plant varieties. Protection is granted for a minimum of 15 years to plant varieties that are stable, homogenous, and clearly distinguishable from other varieties. Farmer's and research exemptions apply, allowing farmers to harvest and replant seeds and researchers to experiment with and improve the new varieties.

must first take IP disputes to the WTO's Dispute Settlement Body (DSB), rather than resorting to unilateral threats or sanctions. An impartial panel is then set up to judge whether the agreements have been reasonably interpreted and carried out. If not, possible remedies include orders to stop the infringing practice, the destruction of infringing goods, or the assessment of monetary damages.

Another innovation that makes TRIPs unique is the obligation countries have under it to enforce intellectual property rights both within the domestic markets and at their borders. TRIPs makes nations responsible for preventing the export of infringing goods from their territories.

Ratification of the NAFTA and TRIPs agreements was a victory for American innovators. The two put in place a framework for the international management of intellectual property that comes very close to the standards of protection advocated by the advanced industrialized countries. IP thus metamorphosed from a purely national policy for promoting investments in new ideas and technologies into a mechanism for spreading the cost of research and development over all economies. These agreements made intellectual property rights a multilateral trade issue. It is a mistake, however, to assume that American IP battles are over.

TRIPs' Weaknesses

TRIPs has numerous weaknesses and loopholes that are unacceptable to the United States.[38] The most objectionable are the long transition periods granted to developing countries: some products will not receive IP protection in the least-developed countries until the year 2010. Worse, countries self-select whether they are de-

---

[38] For a fuller description of industry's reservations, see the Industry Functional Advisory Committee on Intellectual Property Rights, "Report to the Congress on the Uruguay Round," January 10, 1994.

veloped, developing, or least developed, and so decide at what pace they will institute changes to their IP regimes. The developed countries had to implement changes one year after the WTO's inception (by January 1, 1996), while developing countries were granted a five-year transition period, and the least developed a ten-year transition. The benefits of a strong global IP system will thus not be fully realized until after the millennium.

Other complaints focus on the exceptions and derogations from the TRIPs standards of protection, such as the exclusion of recombinant DNA technologies and Internet publications, which the United States would like to see eliminated. Many U.S. companies are also disappointed that TRIPs still permits some compulsory licensing of intellectual property. Finally, TRIPs leaves unresolved such complicated questions as what constitutes international exhaustion of intellectual property rights and how "nullification and impairment" cases will be handled. [39]

Intellectual property disputes would not disappear from the trade scene even if the United States were satisfied with the level of protection afforded by TRIPs. We are living through an era of rapid technological evolution that fundamentally influences how we understand products, processes, and ideas.[40] Twenty years ago nobody thought of genotype as property; electrical signals were

---

[39] Geographic exhaustion refers to the ability of a title holder to prevent the importation of a product that is based on his or her intellectual property. TRIPs leaves the decision of whether a title holder has the ability to block importation to the individual nations. There has been much heated debate on this issue, even among the advanced industrialized countries. There is a five-year moratorium on "nullification and impairment" cases, in which a country that has abided by the letter of the law is nevertheless accused of nullifying or impeding the rights holder's ability to benefit from his intellectual property through behaviors not covered by the WTO.

[40] For an excellent discussion of the attempts made by the U.S. IP system to adapt to new technologies, see John H. Barton, "Adapting the Intellectual Property System to New Technologies," in National Research Council, *Global Dimensions of Intellectual Property Rights in Science and Technology*, Washington, D.C., National Academy Press, 1993.

not the equivalent of paper copies; software was considered text, not invention.[41] Now countries and interest groups within countries fight over the definition of ownership in these slippery fields.[42] The number of court cases dealing with software patents and biotechnology indicates that, domestically, the United States has not fully resolved how to protect the newest technologies. At the international level, where different values and traditions are added to the uncertainty over how to treat novel technologies, one can expect a consensus to form even more slowly.

The interests of developing countries also militate against a quick resolution of international IP tensions. For the advanced industrialized countries, there is little controversy over the notion that stronger global rights will help firms recoup investments in research and development. In the developing world, however, the welfare effects of stronger intellectual property rights need much more study. Recent studies are beginning to confirm the U.S. position that stronger IP systems increase trade flows and attract foreign direct investment.[43] Empirical evidence should soon emerge from Mexico, Chile, and Brazil—the newly industrializing coun-

---

[41] Information technology is especially problematic. The Clinton administration report "Intellectual Property and the National Information Infrastructure" represents one attempt to create "a domestic and international norms for intellectual property protection" on the Internet. How to define ownership on the Internet and for databases is a highly contested national problem. In biology the patentability of gene fragments is a similarly contested topic. And while surgical and medical procedures are patentable, recent attempts to collect fees for such patented procedures have caused an uproar.

[42] For a discussion of the difficulty of protection in pharmaceuticals, see Bale, "Regionalism and the Protection of IPRs," and in biotechnology see Kate Murashige, "Industrial Policy and Biotechnology—Can Intellectual Property Protection Systems Catch Up?" unpublished paper for the Council on Foreign Relations study group American IPR Policy after the TRIPs Agreement, March 1996.

[43] See Mansfield, "Intellectual Property Protection, Foreign Direct Investment, and Technology Transfer," and Maskus, "Regionalism and Protection of IPRs."

tries that have recently enacted stronger IP laws.[44] But in less-developed countries where the main policy objective is often economic growth, a faster rate of diffusion of new ideas is probably more important than a strong IP system that fosters domestic innovation.[45] A more socialist tradition of government intervention on behalf of consumers works against aligning IP systems with the standards of the First World in countries like India, Indonesia, and Egypt.

One theory holds that as countries develop, the level of intellectual property rights protection also rises. The Latin American experience seems to lend credence to the belief that time and wealth lead to robust IPRs. Yet the transition is not automatic, and many contend that external pressure is necessary to push IPRs onto the trade agenda in the first place.[46] For example, without U.S. insistence, IPRs would not have been an important part of the Uruguay Round, and China would have waited far longer to upgrade its IP laws. The tension between the domestic desire for stronger IP and the catalyzing role of foreign pressure suggests that disputes will continue to flare up. They may even get worse. As the market power and political clout of China and India continue to expand, for example, their autonomy with respect to the United States may make them less sensitive to U.S. demands. The eventual decline of American influence gives the United States

---

[44] For an interesting perspective from Mexico, see Antonio Medina Mora Icaza, "The Mexican Software Industry," in the National Research Council, *Global Dimensions of Intellectual Property Rights in Science and Technology* ,Washington, D.C.: National Academy Press, 1992.

[45] For a discussion of the importance of ideas and technologies to growth in developing countries, see Paul Romer, "Two Strategies for Economic Development: Using Ideas and Producing Ideas," Proceedings of the World Bank Annual Conference on Development Economics 1992, Washington, D.C.: World Bank, 1993, pp. 63–91.

[46] Carlos Primo Braga made this argument for Brazil, and Harvey Bale for pharmaceutical protection.

great incentive to insist strongly on changes in these two economies as soon as possible.

Because TRIPs is incomplete, technology continues to change,
and important developing countries remain unconvinced of the
value of a strong IP system, the United States should expect repeated rounds of IP negotiations in the future. The TRIPs agreement was a successful solution for problems faced in the 1980s,
but it is not a permanent panacea for global IP disputes. It built a
multilateral framework, but did not remove the incentives to unilateral and bilateral solutions that the United States finds so
tempting. With a panoply of unilateral, plurilateral, and multilateral tools at its disposal, the United States will continue to push
countries beyond TRIPs commitments. The achievements of
TRIPs are considerable, and the United States should try first and
foremost to build on them and expand the multilateral IP system.
However, the relevant policy question here is what the United
States wants to achieve and what the best means are to those ends.

But before turning to policy options, the United States needs to
understand who the modern pirates are and why separating them
from their booty will not be an easy task. Only then can it sketch
realistic blueprints for the construction of the next stage in global
IP protection.

THE MODERN PIRATES

THE MOST IMPORTANT REASONS intellectual property disputes are here to stay are that modern piracy is big business and that stopping piracy requires behind-the-border intervention in national policies, which is politically difficult.

Every year a few dozen countries are cited by the U.S. Trade Representative for their lack of vigilance in intellectual property.[47] Factories abroad churn out millions of copies of illegal products for both domestic and, more worrisome, international markets. A 1993 USTR report suggested that U.S. entrepreneurs lose up to $60 billion annually from infringement of their intellectual property, and some estimates of American losses to piracy run as high as $200 billion annually.[48]

Of course, damages are difficult to estimate because they seek to measure what was not sold and the profits not made.[49] In calculating losses one must estimate how much of a country's market would have been captured in the absence of infringing products,

---

[47] In 1996 the United States placed China, Argentina, the European Union, Greece, India, Indonesia, Japan, Korea, and Turkey on the "priority foreign countries list" or the "priority watch list." An additional two dozen countries are on the "watch list" for questionable IP practices.

[48] Office of the U.S. Trade Representative, *The Uruguay Round: Growth for the World, Jobs for the U.S.—A Primer*, Dec. 1, 1993, p. 6. As quoted in Richard Steinberg, "The Uruguay Round: A Preliminary Analysis of the Final Act," Laws of International Trade, February 1994. The U.S. International Trade Commission estimated the aggregate worldwide losses to infringement at $23.8 billion for key U.S. sectors in 1986. See U.S. ITC, *Foreign Protection of Intellectual Property Rights and Its Effect on U.S. Industry and Trade—Report to the U.S. Trade Representative*, Investigation no. 332–245, Publication no. 2065, Washington, D.C., 1988.

[49] Business associations, the U.S. government, and foreign governments each use different assumptions to calculate lost sales or lost profits.

and at what price.[50] Industrywide figures are rare. According to an International Trade Commission report, in 1986 the software and computer industries lost $4.1 billion to infringement. The scientific and photographic equipment industries estimated lost sales of $5.1 billion. The pharmaceutical, entertainment, motor vehicle, and electronics industries each lost about $2 billion. Chemicals and petroleum refining lost $1.3 billion each. The total damages from worldwide lost sales, according to the ITC, amounted to $24 billion.[51] Most individual industries' estimates for current losses are significantly larger.

While the cumulative figures are impressive, even more significant is the fact that infringement makes market entry into countries whose economies are growing very difficult. In addition, the United States fears that pirated goods are then exported, cutting into the market share of legitimate products in third countries. For precisely these reasons, the United States was adamant in the spring of 1996 that China shut down 31 pirate factories—the majority of them joint ventures with Taiwanese and Hong Kong companies—and increase customs control. China had the capacity to make fifteen times more CDs, LDs, and CD-ROMs than are purchased domestically. [52] Obviously most products were destined

---

[50] Frequently companies must adjust their prices to the purchasing power of the developing world if they are to compete at all. In calculating lost sales or profits, therefore, one cannot use the price of the product in the home market, but must estimate how much it could sell for in the developing country and how large a market it could then command. When calculating damages due to infringement, courts resort to one of several metrics, including: "(1) the intellectual property owner's actual economic loss caused by the infringement; (2) the infringer's total profits derived from the infringement; or (3) an amount no less than a reasonable royalty." See Jianyang Yu, "Protection of Intellectual Property in the PRC," *Pacific Basin Law Journal,* vol. 13, no. 140 (1994), pp. 140–62.

[51] USITC Publication 2065, 1988, "Foreign Protection of Intellectual Property Rights and the Effect on U.S. Industry and Trade," Washington, D.C.

[52] USTR, "Chinese IPR Piracy Results in Fewer Jobs for U.S. Workers," USTR Fact Sheet, January 5, 1995.

for wider Asian markets. To prevent such "double whammy" revenue erosion, the United States now believes border controls are key to new intellectual property agreements.

Hardest hit by intellectual property infringement are the high-technology sectors and the entertainment industries. Not all are victims of the same type of infringement, however. Counterfeiting is the illegal copying of brand-name products or the use of a trademark without the permission of its owner. Levi's jeans, BMW spare parts, and Whitney Houston CDs are frequently counterfeited. The pirate, on the other hand, illegally uses a copyrighted or patented product or process. In piracy, retaining name recognition may not be central to profitability—as with many pirate pharmaceutical and agrochemical products. Finally, the most subtle type of infringement occurs when an idea, a product, or a process is similar to, improves on, or incorporates another patented or copyrighted product without the permission or remuneration of the rights holder. The conditions under which this use constitutes infringement are often contestable. In many cases, determining whether infringement has occurred at all requires a great deal of technical knowledge, and leads to fierce disputes, domestic as well as international.

Unfortunately for the advanced industrialized world, IP infringement is easy and relatively cheap. Pirates are hard to eradicate because they are frequently small companies with low overhead costs and capital requirements, which when shut down quickly reopen elsewhere or are replaced by new entrants. Modern technologies are conspiring to make protection even more difficult. Rapid access to and replication of new ideas and products is made simple by personal computers, the Internet, and low-cost but high-performance equipment like new-generation copier machines. In China, computer disks containing up to $20,000 worth of stolen software can be bought for a few dollars. Moreover, companies that want to hide their infringing activities can render pirated software programs unrecognizable over the course of a couple of days using simple algorithms to transform the program code.[53] Many pharmaceuticals that required hundreds of millions of dollars to research and develop are trivial to synthesize.[54] Knockoff drugs sell in developing markets at one-tenth to one-fifth the cost charged when licensed from the inventor.[55]

In addition, the built-in lead time that companies used to enjoy, which allowed them a certain period of market exclusivity, has disappeared. Product cycles in most industries have shrunk due to a more targeted approach to research and growing consensus over which products and markets to pursue.[56] Combined with the rapidity of modern travel and communications, the transfer of know-how from country to country is almost instantaneous: copies of the computer operating system Windows 95 were on the streets of Moscow and Beijing before they hit New York.

While pirates can be found in all corners of the globe, the United States is most concerned with the big emerging markets (BEMs), primarily in Asia and Latin America. (Less-developed countries have little capacity to purchase or absorb new technologies and are, in the medium term, almost irrelevant to U.S. IP interests. The advanced industrialized countries are already signatories to the important IP conventions and well integrated into the

---

[53] William T. Ellis, "Patent and Copyright Protection for Software in the Post TRIPs World," unpublished paper for Council on Foreign Relations study group, *American IPR Policy after the TRIPs Agreement*, March 1996.

[54] The Pharmaceutical Manufacturers and Research Association estimates that the costs of developing a drug—initial research to marketplace—are between $300 million and $500 million for a U.S. firm; see Kate Murashige, "Industrial Policy and Biotechnology—Can Intellectual Property Protection Systems Catch Up?"

[55] See Daniel Pearl, "Big Drug Makers Push Egypt, Other Nations to End their Piracy," *The Wall Street Journal*, December 13, 1996, p. A1.

[56] Harvey Bale makes the point that most pharmaceutical research has become narrowly targeted on key diseases such as AIDS, heart disease, and cancer, see Bale, "Regionalism and the Protection of IPRs."

international system.[57]) The emerging markets, on the other hand, promise an ever growing, ever richer consumer base for IP products (see Table 2). They are large countries, accounting for one-half of the world's population, whose purchasing power is rapidly expanding.

The importance of the BEMs as present and future markets cannot be overstated. One-quarter of U.S. exports in 1994 were to the BEM countries. By the turn of the century, ITC projections put the BEM share at one-half of U.S. exports.[58] BEM growth rates, on the whole, are substantially higher than the world average of 2.9 per cent, with some Asian BEMs growing three times more rapidly. [59] It is expected that their GDP will double over the next 20 years, and that by 2020 six of the ten largest economies will be BEMs.[60] These countries have undertaken economic programs to increase growth, trade, and investment. In Asia especially, poverty rates are dropping, while exports and productivity are on the rise. Spending on health care, software, and entertainment is bound to rise also. Clearly, the advanced industrialized countries would like to bring this large segment of humanity into the fold of the international trade system.

Not only do these countries represent future markets, but some are also producers of more advanced technology products, with a significant strata of scientists and the potential to spawn high-

---

[57] This is not to say that the U.S. is not concerned with IP infringement domestically or in advanced countries. Advanced countries are reviewed by the USTR on an ongoing basis. The eight trading partners placed on the "priority watch list" in April 1996 included, for example, the European Union, Japan, and Greece. On the watch list were Italy, Canada, Japan, and Australia.

[58] See Jeffrey Garten, "The Big Emerging Markets," *Columbia Journal of World Business,* vol. 31, no. 2 (Summer 1996), pp. 6–31.

[59] Average annual GDP growth rates for the world from 1980–1993. See World Bank, *Workers in an Integrating World,* New York: Oxford University Press, 1995, pp. 164–65.

[60] Garten, "The Big Emerging Markets."

technology industries. Brazil, for example, is known for its informatics industry, India for its software companies, and Argentina and, increasingly, Egypt for their pharmaceutical production. As Keith Maskus documents, trade in high-tech goods, which now accounts for over 50 percent of total merchandise trade for the developed countries, is growing even more rapidly in developing countries. [61] In Mexico, 42 percent of merchandise trade in 1993 was in high tech goods, a figure that had nearly quadrupled since 1985. In Korea, high-tech goods accounted for 45 percent of merchandise trade, and in China, 35 percent; in both countries growth rates of technology products since 1985 have roughly doubled.[62] The United States is therefore taking a keen interest in shaping the terms of competition with the BEMs because they represent growing technology markets and future competitors.

The big emerging markets are also big entertainment markets. Piracy in the $40 billion worldwide music industry is estimated to be $2 billion annually and growing.[63] Brazil's legal music industry has revenues of $700 million, 84 percent of which is dominated by affiliates of Northern multinational companies.[64] Piracy is a problem in Brazil, but not on the order of China, which produces an estimated $250 million of pirated music CDs and cassettes every

---

[61] Maskus, "Regionalism and the Protection of IPRs."

[62] Figures for 1985–93, from Maskus, "Regionalism and the Protection of IPRs."

[63] Figures from the International Federation of the Phonographic Industry. See Frances Williams, "Copyright rules planned for the Internet," *Financial Times*, December 2, 1996, p. 4.

[64] See John Lannert, "Latin Notas," *Billboard*, February 24, 1996.

Table 2. Population, per capita GNP, and GDP growth rates in the 10 BEMs

	Population (millions), 1993	GNP per capita (PPP), 1993	GDP annual growth 1980–93
Argentina	34	$8250	0.8%
Brazil	157	$5370	2.1%
China (PRC)	1,178	$2300	9.6%
India	898	$1220	5.2%
Indonesia	187	$3150	5.8%
Mexico	90	$6810	1.6%
Poland	38	$5000	0.7%
South Africa	40	n.a.	0.9%
South Korea	44	$9630	9.1%
Thailand	58	$6260	8.2%
Turkey	60	$5160	4.6%
U.S.	**258**	**$24,740**	**2.7%**

Source: World Bank, *Workers in an Integrating World*, Oxford University Press: New York, 1995. U.S. figures for comparison.

year and where three-quarters of all music CDs are pirated.[65] In the film industry, the fastest growing market is Asia. India already has a $1 billion movie industry, which produces two times as

---

[65] See Shada Islam, "Foreign Record Companies Have a Deal for China," *Far Eastern Economic Review*, November 21, 1996, pp. 84–86. Note that the losses to bootlegged, counterfeit, and pirate recordings in the U.S. amount to $300 million a year according to the Recording Industry Association of America. See Don Steinberg, "Digital Underground," *Wired*, no.1 (January 1997), pp. 104–10.

many films as in the United States.[66] Hollywood is interested in augmenting its Indian sales, especially as the country's 13,000 theaters expand in number and raise their 65¢ admission fees. (There is room to grow, as the United States, with one-third India's population, has 29,000 screens.) The greatest growth market is China, which has only 3,000 official cinemas and still regulates foreign film releases. The music, film, and television industries are eager to tap into these fertile markets.

Because of, or perhaps in spite of, their technological ability and their relative affluence, the BEMs are home to some of the world's most virulent pirate producers.[67] In software, 80 percent to 90 percent of all applications in the developing countries are illegally copied (with the exception of Latin American countries, where the figures are somewhat lower). The business software industry estimates that it loses $8 billion to piracy worldwide, an amount equal to its total sales. [68] Piracy rates are generally higher in the developing world, which is why the issue is often portrayed as a North-South problem. But it is important to remember that advanced countries are often responsible for larger total losses due to piracy because their purchasing power is so much greater. High copyright piracy rates in the developed world, for example, are due primarily to higher expenditures on software.[69] It is the rates of piracy, and the lack of prosecution or enforcement, rather than

---

[66] See Sharon Moshavi, "Bollywood Breaks into the Big Time," *Business Week*, September 25, 1995, pp. 122–23.

[67] While piracy is often portrayed as a North–South issue because piracy rates are much higher in developing nations, in fact the gross estimates of piracy losses are much larger for the industrialized countries because their purchasing power is so much greater. It is the rates of piracy, and the lack of prosecution or enforcement, which makes infringement most problematic in the BEMs.

[68] See Software Publishers Association, *1995 Report on Global Software Piracy*, Washington, D.C., 1995.

[69] According to the IIPA, software piracy accounts for 77% and 84% of copyright piracy losses in Europe and the United States, respectively.

Table 3. Estimated losses due to global copyright piracy, 1994

	Piracy Losses (millions of U.S. $)	World Percentage
Western Europe	3809.2	25.50
United States and Canada	3517.0	23.55
Developing Asia Pacific	2296.2	15.37
Japan, Hong Kong, Singapore	1531.5	10.25
Russia and CIS, East Europe	1462.0	9.79
South and Latin America	1442.2	9.66
Middle East, Mediterranean	773.5	5.18
Africa	103.7	0.70
Total	**14,935.3**	**100.00%**

Source: International Intellectual Property Alliance.

the absolute value of losses that make infringement most problematic in the BEMs.

The United States is immediately concerned with piracy in Asia and Latin America.[70] Contemporary Latin America, however, is less problematic than Asia. A greater percentage of losses in films, music, software, and, especially, print occur in Asia than in Latin America.[71] Computer chip theft in Asia is reputed to run to $8 bil-

---

[70] For a discussion of developing country IP issues see Carlos Alberto Primo Braga, "The Newly Industrializing Economies," in M. Wallerstein, M.E. Mogee, and R. Schoen, *Global Dimensions of Intellectual Property Rights in Science and Technology,* Washington, D.C.: National Academy Press, 1993.

[71] IIPA, "Copyright Industries in the U.S. Economy: 1977–1993."

lion a year.[72] In addition, the ratification of NAFTA, the new economic liberalism, and an increased sensitivity to the desires of foreign direct investors has set Latin American nations on a course of IPR reform, the latest step of which was the enactment of Brazil's new and modern patent law in April 1996. The MERCOSUR grouping—Brazil, Argentina, Paraguay, and Uruguay—adopted a common protocol for trademarks in 1995, and discussions on copyrights are under way. Similarly, the Free Trade Area of the Americas created a Working Group on Intellectual Property Rights at its meeting in Colombia early this year. With the exception of Argentina, all indications are that Latin America is committed to establishing stronger IP standards unilaterally and through regional cooperation.[73]

Asian countries have not been bitten by the same IPR bug that is driving Latin American reforms. In particular, the People's Republic of China, not yet a WTO signatory, poses huge enforcement problems, making it the only country in 1996 for which the United States considered trade sanctions to force IP changes. One rung down the USTR's hierarchy, three of the five BEMs on the "priority watch list" in 1996 were in Asia.[74] India's lack of modern patent and trademark laws, and its delay in passing legislation for the TRIPs mandated "mailbox" for filing pharmaceutical and agricultural patents, raises the possibility of a WTO violation.[75] Indo-

---

[72] In a semiconductor chip market worth $151 billion, most of the theft occurs within Asia. See Emily Thornton, "Some Like it Hot," *Far Eastern Economic Review*, August 15, 1996, pp. 58–60.

[73] Despite earlier assurances and efforts on the part of the Argentine president, the Argentine legislature enacted a new patent law in 1995 which fell short of the protection required under the TRIPs agreement.

[74] The other BEMs were Argentina and Turkey. Non-BEMs European Union and Greece were also cited.

[75] Developing countries that do not immediately extend patent protection to pharmaceuticals and agrochemicals must create a mailbox or black box system in which patent applications can be filed so as to be eligible for protection when patent protection is finally extended.

nesia was placed on the USTR's priority watch list for copyright violations. South Korea, which has made great progress in IPRs over the past decade, is on the priority watch list for its lack of trade secret, software, and textile design protection. The USTR even cites Japan, despite its comparatively strong IP rights, for narrow interpretation of patents that spurs companies to "patent-flood," for its treatment of software, and for its lax recording rights.[76]

Raising standards in the greater Asian economic area poses a special challenge to the United States. The APEC regional agreement is broader and weaker than NAFTA, and is therefore unlikely to push significant improvements on the TRIPs agreement. Furthermore, India is located in South Asia and thus not included in either APEC or ASEAN, nor in any other regional grouping headed by one of the advanced industrialized countries. There is no regional trade agreement in Asia that is weaving a strong and inclusive IP net. As Asia represents the fastest growing and most technically endowed of the U.S. developing country trade partners, this region must be a top priority for U.S. policymakers. Asia is an important test case for the question of whether regional or multilateral mechanisms can be used to raise IP standards further.

---

[76] Patent flooding refers to the practice of filing many patents to surround a single innovation with strong protection.

STOPPING PIRACY BEHIND BORDERS—THE CHINA CASE

CERTAINLY, THE TASK of stopping piracy in Asia is daunting. The recent showdown with the People's Republic of China illustrates how difficult extinguishing IP infringement actually is. China represents the most challenging case politically for the United States: it is a booming market with great technological potential but is not well integrated into the international trading system. Most important, China is not a member of the WTO. China, however, is no different than Indonesia, India, Argentina, or Turkey in that, in all cases, the United States needs first to establish a legally enforceable agreement and the enactment of domestic IP laws, and second, to encourage their incorporation into the business culture. The behind-the-borders enforcement of new IP agreements is the biggest challenge to U.S. strategy.

In the post-Mao era, China came to recognize the rights of individuals and companies to hold intellectual property and implemented an impressive array of reforms—promulgating laws and joining the major international conventions.[77] But the pace of change was unsatisfactory to the United States, especially in copyright protection, and three Sino-American IP agreements were negotiated to smooth relations. The first, called the Memorandum of Understanding (MOU) on Intellectual Property Rights, was signed in 1992 and established strong legal foundations for domestic IP

---

[77] For an overview of the recent Chinese IPR reforms, see Michel Oksenberg, Pitman Potter, and William Abnett, "Advancing Intellectual Property Rights: Information Technologies and the Course of Economic Development in China," in *NBR Analysis*, The National Bureau of Asian Research, vol. 7, no. 4, November 1996.

protection. While on paper the MOU created an exemplary intellectual property rights system, the laws did not guarantee enforcement. Through 1993 and 1994, the United States presented China with evidence of violations, sometimes including the names and addresses of companies blatantly ignoring China's new IP laws. U.S. complaints culminated in February 1995 with the threat of $1 billion in sanctions if China did not agree to the following three measures: (1) shut down and prosecute domestic infringers, (2) halt exports of infringing goods at the border, and (3) open the Chinese market to legal U.S. movies, sound recordings, and computer software.[78] Tensions with the United States were high, but Beijing capitulated at the last minute and a second agreement—the 1995 IPR Enforcement Agreement—unequivocally laid out what steps the PRC would take to abide by the earlier Memorandum of Understanding.

The story, as we know, did not end in 1995. The United States continued to monitor China's commitments, sending delegation after delegation to Beijing and the provinces to discuss IP violations. Under U.S. pressure, China conducted over 4,000 raids, destroying millions of pirated CDs, videos, audiocassettes, and counterfeit trademark products.[79] China's emphasis, however, was on prosecuting the domestic retail sector rather than the manufacturers. So in spite of government raids, exports of pirated goods continued. From the U.S. perspective, Beijing was again not enforcing its IP agreements. In May 1996 USTR designated China a "priority foreign country" under Section 301, and threatened $2.3 billion of retaliatory tariffs to make up for lost American sales. China immediately countered with its own proposed sanctions. A

---

[78] The stipulations of the 1995 U.S. IPR Enforcement Agreement are drawn from a USTR Fact Sheet, "Intellectual Property Rights Enforcement in China," May 1996.

[79] Ibid.

frenzied exchange of delegates criss-crossed the Pacific, and at the last moment, a joint declaration averted a trade war.

Through negotiations and threats, the United States succeeded in getting the Chinese government to establish stronger intellectual property rights, but not in rapidly changing the behavior of either the government or the pirates. The second stage in endingan end to piracy requires creating a domestic constituency that supports intellectual property rights. Often, even if adequate IP laws are on the books, weak legal institutions and culture mean that many people are unaware of the prohibitions on IP use or do not to take them seriously.[80] In China, the legal culture problem is exacerbated by government officials who are themselves involved in the pirate trade. An inflammatory article in *Wired* translates a discussion with a young Chinese man, Ye Sang, known as one of the "Four Heavenly Kings of Hacking," who works in Beijing's Thieves Alley. Ye, who is in his early twenties, is not impressed with U.S. attempts to halt software piracy:

> "They can hit China with as many sanctions as they want. Besides, they're only punishing the central government; it can't touch any of us. At least the foreign devils got that right—the Chinese government is the one to go after. Boy they make a heap from pirating! I couldn't copy programs for heavy-duty machines, even if I wanted to. I don't have any originals to work with, nor do I have the know-how, equipment, or access to a market. I've got no alternative but to let the government make the real [financial] killing.
>
> "The government raided us a few days ago, just to give the Yanks some face during the latest round of Sino-U.S. intellectual property talks. Go for it! All they got was a few disks. We still have software coming out our ears. Our [police] were just putting on a show for the

---

[80] See William P. Alford, *To Steal a Book Is an Elegant Offense,* Stanford: Stanford University Press, 1995.

Yankee devils. If they really wanted to enforce a ban, they'd hit the National Defense Science, Technology, and Industry Commission or the Academy of Sciences. All we get are their leftovers. The government has been breaking the same laws we have. If they don't give a damn, why should we be scared?"[81]

The lack of a strong stand by top officials on IPRs, the divided bureaucratic responsibility for IPRs, and the divide between the central government and local officials is sending mixed messages to pirates and has complicated enforcement efforts.[82] It is not surprising, therefore, that over 95 percent of all computer software in China is pirated, compared to 30 percent in the United States.[83]

The PRC's desire to accede to the WTO has aided the U.S. position in negotiations. The United States wants consistent TRIP protection as one prerequisite to endorsing China's membership. The battle has been over the content of legislation as overenforcement of adequate existing copyright laws. The United States is insisting that China immediately guarantee IP protection—even though developing nations that were founding members of the WTO were allowed a five-to-ten-year transition period. Because China is such an important BEM, the United States wants it to go "cold turkey." In March 1997 China announced it would not seek a transition period if it were admitted to the WTO.

Intellectual property protection disagreements have strained relations with China. It could have been worse, however. Sino-American disputes focus on the copyright industries. The most acrimonious North-South battles are over patents, as the standoffs

---

[81] Sang Ye, "Computer Insect," *Wired*, no. 4.7 p. 82.

[82] For an elaboration of the domestic politics of IP protection, see Oksenberg, Potter, and Abnett, "Advancing Intellectual Property Rights: Information Technologies and the Course of Economic Development in China."

[83] Figures from Software Publishers Association, *1995 Report on Global Software Piracy*, Washington, D.C.

with India and Argentina testify. The problem with patents is that pharmaceuticals and agrochemicals were granted the longest transition periods in TRIPs, because developing countries feel strongly that IP protection for such vital products is against the public interest, while advanced countries insist that without it, the ills that plague developing countries will go unheeded by science.

China illustrates the problems inherent in both reaching an IP agreement with a developing country and subsequently creating a domestic base for stronger IP rights. But while China has been in the news most recently, it is far from being the lone infringer. Each continent has its share of piracy, with a large number of Asian nations—including South Korea, Taiwan, Thailand, Hong Kong, Indonesia, Vietnam, and India—having been cited by the U.S. government for IP infringement. Eventually 150 nations will be signatories to the WTO, to abide by the minimum standards of IP protection. For the U.S. IP strategy, the adoption of IP laws overseas is the first and easiest step in a plan to create strong protection internationally. The hard part, as made perfectly clear in China, is the implementation: the monitoring and enforcement of IP statutes. Creating domestic interest in stronger IP rights is hard to achieve through simple trade pressure. In challenging Asian IP practices, U.S. strategy must take into account the subtleties of behind-the-border implementation.

AMERICAN GOALS

THE CHALLENGES TO STRONG, global IP rights are easy to identify: recalcitrance in the big emerging markets, the difficulty of behind-the-border monitoring and enforcement of IP agreements, and the emergence of new technologies that challenge existing concepts of intellectual property. Less easy to pin down are American objectives. Ideally, the United States would like global intellectual property protection of a breadth and strength equivalent to that available in the United States, and judicial systems capable of enforcing the letter of the law. [84] American officials would be much happier if more IP regimes resembled that of the United States, and this guides U.S. IP rhetoric and policies.

But a global intellectual property system that mirrors the U.S. model is unrealistic for others. To begin with, the American IPR system has quirks that the rest of the developed world does not share or want. Most prominent is the convention of establishing

---

[84] Breadth refers to the number of product and process categories covered in the IP system. Even in countries with relatively strong IP systems, products like pharmaceuticals and recombinant plants or animals often have not received IP protection because governments believe that public interest dictates that drugs and food be available at reasonable prices or because such IP protection would violate public order or morality. The strength of patent protection includes the length of time the protection is offered (e.g., 20-year patent terms, 50-year copyright terms plus life of the author) and the ease with which one can defend the protection from infringers. The United States, for example, has long claimed that Japan's protection is weak because it does not have a doctrine of equivalents and tends to narrowly interpret patent claims. In Japan, if the claims in two separate applications do not literally infringe, competitors are allowed to make similar products; in the United States, the courts would hold that if the products perform substantially the same function in substantially the same way, the second product would infringe.

priority by the date of invention rather than the date of filing.[85] American firms themselves are not eager to export some peculiarities of the U.S. system, such as overly broad patent coverage and the expensive litigiousness of intellectual property disputes.[86]

The main obstacle to a harmonization of U.S. norms, however, is the fact that a country's intellectual property regime is a central part of its research and development system. Each nation's IP regime consists of a series of trade-offs between producers and consumers, inventors and improvers, and even between generations. Advanced countries bicker about the details of how to strike a balance between interest groups, and developing countries, which often favor the consumer, improvers, and the present generation, are even warier of harmonization to an American standard. Every IP regime presents a series of fundamental choices about the amount spent on development, the type of research that is economically viable, and the rate at which new technologies spread through society.[87] The natural desire of individual countries to maintain control over their R&D policy makes it difficult for the United States to pursue harmonization to the U.S. norm—or, for that matter, to make any other country's IP system the standard.

The United States cannot re-create the world in its image, but it has not identified alternatives either. Part of the uncertainty over how to proceed since the ratification of TRIPs stems from an American aversion to admitting that there are choices, each with

---

[85] While the "first to invent" system in the United States more accurately reflects who came up with an invention, the "first to file" system used by most other countries is easier to administer. At the prodding of Europe and Japan, the United States is considering harmonizing to the de facto world standard.

[86] The consensus within industry is that patent coverage is much too broad and blocks the ability of later developers to use the technology. In the biotechnology field, for example, profits from 30% of sales go to pay legal expenses in disputes, most often to protect a company's intellectual property.

[87] Take Japan and the United States. The two are at an equivalent stage of development, but the choices they have made for IP protection are very different and have heavily influenced their national innovative capabilities.

pros and cons and each implying different commitments and strategies on the part of the United States. In order to create a consensus, to proceed rationally, and to win developing countries' commitment to higher levels of protection, clearer U.S. objectives are needed.

As a first step, we can identify two very general points on which American industry and government agree: (1) stronger global IPRs are desirable and should be pursued, and (2) all efforts should be made to minimize any loss of sovereignty over our domestic intellectual property rights system. Given these two tenets, the United States is aiming for a fixed minimum level of protection to which all countries must agree and which theoretically allows for variation among developmental strategies. The United States must narrow its goals still further, choosing between a simple enforcement of TRIPs on the one hand and a deep harmonization of national IPR systems on the other.

TRIPs Enforcement

The most conservative goal is simply to monitor and enforce existing IP agreements. Without doubt, making sure that countries fully implement TRIPs would substantially raise standards above present levels. If tomorrow there could be complete implementation of TRIPs, most U.S. firms would be very satisfied. But in terms of U.S. policy, this option is essentially the status quo. The showdown with China during the spring of 1996 was precisely about compelling the PRC to monitor and enforce its own laws. And the WTO already has a dispute settlement procedure that reviews countries accused of violating the TRIPs Agreement. The Clinton administration has initiated 20 WTO dispute settlement proceedings, leaving no doubt that the United States will push for strict enforcement of existing agreements. Five cases—against Japan, Portugal, India, Pakistan, and Turkey—involved intellectual property complaints.[88]

Monitoring and enforcement, therefore, are the bottom line strategies for the United States. From a policy perspective, it would require a commitment to and faith in the WTO's dispute settlement mechanism, a desire to bring in countries not yet party to the WTO, and bilateral negotiations to extend TRIPs-like standards to countries unable to accede. However, TRIPs enforcement is unlikely to be our only strategy: TRIPs has too many loopholes and ambiguities to make it acceptable as a permanent solution.

Uniform Global IPRs

The most ambitious goal moves far beyond harmonization to unification of the disparate intellectual property systems. A supranational body would be created and made responsible for the administration and coordination of IPRs. Advantages over the present system are numerous: single applications would lower filing costs; prior art searches for patents would be necessary only once and property rights assigned would be recognized in all member countries.[89] To a degree, elements of a unified system are present in the Patent Cooperation Treaty, the European Patent Office, and other IP conventions that try to simplify international filing. Uni-

---

[88] The case against Japan was filed in February 1996 for "failure to protect the rights of U.S. performing artists and producers who recorded in the 25-year period between 1946 and 1971." See the USTR press release of April 30, 1996, "USTR Announces Two Decisions: Title VII and Special 301." Turkey is cited for its tax on receipts from the showing of foreign films; India and Pakistan because they have not set up a "mailbox" system for pharmaceuticals and agrochemicals; and Portugal because its patent term was inconsistent with TRIPs.

[89] In patent applications, prior art searches are performed (a) to determine whether a patent has already been issued for the product or process, and (b) to make sure that the invention is not already part of the public domain of knowledge and therefore not patentable. In the absence of cooperative agreements, prior art searches must be performed in every country in which the patent application is filed.

fication would coordinate and deepen these various agreements, to create one or several joint and centralized administrative systems. Of course, a unified IP regime raises familiar problems of sovereignty and control over domestic R&D systems. The U.S. Congress would fight any loss of U.S. autonomy, so from the American perspective a prerequisite to unification is harmonization to U.S. standards. This makes unification an ambitious and long-range goal, if feasible at all.

TRIPs-Plus

Somewhere in between enforcing the status quo and creating strong international organizations are options that combine different elements of institutionalism and different levels of standardization. Borrowing a classification scheme from the Brookings Institution, the real choice lies somewhere between further *coordination* of differing national IPR regimes and higher *standardization* levels than embodied in TRIPs.[90] Remember that there is no true international system of intellectual property protection. Domestic IP regimes are overlaid with international agreements about the type and length of protection and enforcement signatory countries agree to provide. In TRIPs-plus, national IP systems remain distinct, but standards and norms could be negotiated in a multi-nation context to create greater congruence between individual IP systems (minimizing differences among national IP re-

---

[90] The Brookings Institution publishes a series entitled "Integrating National Economies." The editors distinguish between six levels of international convergence: national autonomy, mutual recognition, mutual decentralization, coordination, explicit harmonization, and federalist mutual governance. I believe that international IP protection has already attained a significant degree of coordination. The question facing WTO members—and participants in WIPO or other IP agreements—is whether further harmonization is possible, or even whether federalist mutual governance is feasible and desirable. The relevant volume here is Miles Kahler, *International Institutions and the Political Economy of Integration,* Washington, D.C.: The Brookings Institution, 1995.

gimes), and standards of protection raised.[91] The objective is a harmonization of laws and a gradual ratcheting-up of international IPRs.

The standards options is a middle road between a conservative strategy and actually creating a supranational body. It is what most American industries hope the United States will pursue. But the standards option leaves open the level of institutionalism necessary and how much breadth and depth of protection will be demanded. It requires that the United States be more explicit about its goals for the global system. More specifically, it demands consideration of the following issues:

- Level of Protection: What breadth and strength of protection are acceptable as global minimum (legal system, administrative system, border controls, business culture)?

- Subject Categories: New technologies continually challenge the limits of existing intellectual property rights. Which product categories should be considered in the international arena?

- Monitoring and Enforcement: How can the new standards be monitored? Does the United States cede oversight to an international body, or does it protect its ability to act unilaterally to accelerate the changes?

- In how many years does the United States want the transition to occur?

---

[91] Robert Sherwood makes the distinction between creating a single global IP system and making the individual national systems more uniform and congruent. See Robert M. Sherwood, "Why a Uniform Intellectual Property System Makes Sense for the World," in M. Wallerstein, M. E. Mogee, and R. Schoen *Global Dimensions of Intellectual Property Rights in Science and Technology*, Washington, D.C.: National Academy Press, 1993.

- Breadth of Involvement: Which countries should be involved in deeper integration and standardization—all WTO members or a more select few? Why?

- Unification: Are unified, international administrative rules desirable if they reduce costs and simplify interpretation of IPRs? Do the advantages of a unified system outweigh the cost in loss of sovereignty?

There is a surprising degree of agreement in the United States on many of these dimensions. According to the U.S. Trade Representative's office, while an impartial system for dispute resolution is necessary, the United States will retain its right to use sanctions in cases not otherwise covered, as with China, which is not a member of the WTO. Enforcement is the single greatest challenge for stronger global IPRs, as many countries do not have the funds or political will to create the legal and administrative structures to support an IP system. The United States will not abdicate the occasional use of pressure to catalyze change. Given that TRIPs is roundly criticized for its lag time, the timetable for action on intellectual property should be accelerated to well before 2010. A deadline of 2000 for full implementation of TRIPs and a renegotiation of problem areas would be ideal. The U.S. government is very open to regional and bilateral agreements on IPRs. The momentum for sweeping multilateral negotiations is not strong in the mid-1990s, and as we shall see, regional agreements may be more tractable. New technologies should be addressed promptly, but probably not before a consensus has been reached in the United States on how best to protect and promote them. Finally, the creation of supranational offices to oversee or administer intellectual property should be pursued as a long-term goal, rather than a top priority, because of the difficulty of dealing with sovereignty issues.[92]

The U.S. government and its innovating industries want an accelerated TRIPs agreement that includes all the BEMs, strengthens protection for the new technologies, and is enforceable. Unfortunately, this goal is not well articulated either within the government or to U.S. trade partners.

TRIPs-plus necessitates a multitrack approach. First, the United States would rely on the WTO to maintain the basic TRIPs level of protection in most countries. Second, the U.S. would need to negotiate higher levels of protection with specific countries. In all likelihood this will be done outside the WTO framework, in either regional or bilateral forums, as it is unlikely that the United States will be able to get faster implementation or broader protection within the WTO framework in the immediate future. Finally, achieving stronger levels of protection will mean giving something in exchange—be it technology transfer or market access—to win the compliance of the target country. The WTO has placed limitations on U.S. sticks, requiring a greater reliance on carrots to change IP behavior in third countries.

The United States needs to make clear its IP goals. Although muddling through is fine under some circumstances, it is not the optimal strategy for intellectual policy. A consistent, universally applied, and achievable set of goals is necessary because the United States has limited monetary and political resources to

---

[92] However, some supranational organizations are being considered seriously. For example, to decrease the costs of setting up a patent system in developing countries, regional resource sites for prior art searches of already patented innovations are highly recommended.

spend on this particular trade issue. A lack of political momentum for intellectual property issues—at home and abroad—requires that the country choose its battles well.

CONSTRAINTS

IN ADDITION TO unclear goals, recent IP policy has been scatter-shot because American actions are constrained, politically and monetarily. The major impediments to a consistent IP policy include the lack of supportive allies, poor follow-up funding to aid third countries in establishing IP regimes, and weak negotiating tools.

First, intellectual property rights are in one major respect unlike other trade issues: Japan and Europe are not eager to define the international rules. The effort to create a global IP system is driven almost entirely by the United States. Even the successful TRIPs negotiations were in large part pushed by the efforts and enthusiasm of U.S. negotiators and businesses. Since both the Europeans and the Japanese have been much less active in their efforts to change the IP behavior of their trading partners, the first constraint is the lack of supportive allies.

Cooperating with the European Union

The European Union shares many of the American concerns about intellectual property protection in Asia.[93] The high-profile exports of Louis Vuitton handbags, Cognac, EMI classical records, and Mercedes spare parts have high intellectual property content. The overlap of interest is most striking in specific industries. For example, the United States and Europe share world leadership in the

---

[93] Much of this section is adapted from Bénédicte Callan, "The Potential for Co-operation in Intellectual Property in Asia," in Richard Steinberg, ed., *Transatlantic Trade Cooperation in Asia: Issues, Sectors, and Modalities*, unpublished book manuscript.

pharmaceutical and chemical industries.[94] The Europeans have a substantial publishing industry, and sectors such as scientific texts are frequently pirated on international markets. In Europe, the recording industry is even more important than in the United States—three of the top five recording companies are European.[95] The economic impact of piracy is believed to be approximately the same in Europe and the United States, given the equivalent contributions of copyright and high-technology industries to gross domestic product.

Europe, like the United States, sees growth opportunity in dynamic Asian markets and it knows stronger IP regimes would help expand sales to Asia. Its other developing-country export markets—Africa, Eastern and Central Europe, the Middle East—are relatively slow growing. While the percentage of European exports to Asia is still small compared to that of the United States and Japan,[96] the European Commission has made market access and export promotion to Asia a priority.[97] The private sector has obliged, increasing direct investment in Asia fivefold during the early 1990s and rapidly expanding exports. Europe and the United States also share a desire to extend high IP protection to countries outside the WTO, to revise and modernize the TRIPs Agreement, and to make sure that TRIPs is fully implemented by all signatories.

---

[94] Of the largest pharmaceutical firms in 1995, four were European and six were American. However, this distinction makes less and less sense as mergers are bringing Euro-American firms under a single roof.

[95] BMG, EMI, and Polygram are European. The other two are Time Warner (U.S.) and Sony (Japan).

[96] Almost 12% of European exports are to Asia, 14.4% of US and 29.6% of Japanese exports are to Asia. See Frances Williams, "Copyright rules planned for the Internet," *Financial Times*.

[97] Michael Vatikiotis, "Squandered Advantage," *Far Eastern Economic Review*, February 1997.

Government and industry interests, would seem to suggest transatlantic cooperation should be easy. In fact cooperation with third countries has been erratic and fraught with tension. In part the inability to work together in raising IP regimes abroad stems from the fact that there is not a perfect overlap of interests in intellectual property protection. In the packaged software and the motion picture industries, American firms are much larger and more export oriented than their European colleagues. As a result, the Europeans have not been eager to join in U.S. piracy complaints in these areas. But the problems extend beyond simple divergences in industry structure. After all, if the problem was that our concerns were not perfectly parallel, one could imagine a tit-for-tat strategy emerging, in which the United States would agree to back Europe when its interests were most at stake, and vice versa.

Were the Europeans and the Americans to deepen their cooperation, they would need to have not only a common interest in raising IP standards abroad but equivalent strategies for engaging the offending country. Cooperation founders because the United States and Europe disagree about the appropriate modes of action for combating piracy. As the world's largest trading bloc, the EU has considerable influence in making global trade rules. Theoretically, it could be as proactive in shaping IP practices abroad as the United States. But its bilateral tools are far more circumscribed in this arena of trade policy than, for example, those of the United States, and it prefers to rely on multilateral mechanisms for IP dispute resolution. All this has made cooperation outside multilateral frameworks difficult.

Bilaterally, Europe has the greatest influence on the IP regimes of Central and Eastern Europe. The carrot of accession to the EU, however distant, serves as a powerful incentive. Since the minimum standards of accession to the EU are already decided on, there is little bargaining allowed by supplicants. Poland, for example, has upgraded its standards for intellectual property protection, and its piracy rates have dropped considerably since the 1980s. Asia is not Eastern or Central Europe, yet the European Union does have a couple of bilateral tools at its disposal in the East. To begin with, the EU is in the process of renegotiating "Third Generation" framework cooperation agreements with developing countries, which include intellectual property clauses. The European Commission and Korea signed such an agreement in February 1996, in which Korea pledged to implement TRIPs within the year. Korea has made great strides in its compliance with TRIPs. Nepal, Laos, Cambodia, and Vietnam have also concluded framework agreements, while Pakistan, Bangladesh, and India are in the process of negotiating terms. Some agreements have timetables, but most only specify medium-term targets, which are not necessarily binding. In exchange for full implementation of TRIPs, accession to the major IP treaties, and in rare cases higher standards than TRIPs demands, the EU provides technical assistance. While not exacting radical revisions, the framework agreements combine carrots with a vague threat of sticks, thereby articulating Europe's concern about external intellectual property protection.

More powerful is the rarely used Commercial Policy Instrument, akin to Section 301 in the United States, which allows the European Union to take action against its trade partners. The old version, called the New Commercial Policy Instrument (NCPI, 1984), was revised in 1994 as the Trade Barrier Regulation (TBR). Inspired by Section 301 of the 1972 Trade Act in the United States, the European Community decided in 1984 that it should be able to protect its international rights and retaliate against unfair trade practices.[98] But from 1984 to 1994 only four examinations were opened under NCPI and no measures were taken. There are

---

[98] This section is based on Harri Beekmann, "The Revised Commercial Policy Instrument of the European Union," *Law and Economics Review,* Kluwer International: The Hague, 1995.

several reasons for the sparse application of NCPI. First, the northern European countries were wary of its potential for protectionist use. This is ideologically consistent with their dislike of Section 301 as a protectionist unilateral instrument. Second, the requirements for case admissibility were high. The plaintiff had to show injury to a Community industry —not a firm, not a national industry—resulting from an illicit practice. In the United States, the practice simply had to be unfair, and proof of injury to an entire industry was unnecessary. Third, the checks and balances within NCPI made for a slow process in which objections of the member state had to be fully addressed. A member state with important ties to a third country that was under NCPI or TBR investigation could slow or even halt the process if it felt that its other trade or political interests hung in the balance.

Despite its weaknesses, however, the threat of NCPI exacted change in the IP behavior of third countries. In 1984 producers of Scotch whiskey considered filing a case against Bulgaria for its misleading "Scotch Whiskey" products. The Bulgarians dropped the use of the term Scotch before the case could be filed. Two of the four cases that reached the European Commission dealt with piracy: a 1987 case against Indonesia for its piracy in sound recordings, and a similar case in 1991 opened against Thailand in 1991. In bilateral negotiations both countries agreed to change their practice. In 1994 NCPI was revised to work with the dispute resolution mechanism of the WTO. To make it more effective, admissibility requirements were lowered so that simple "obstacles to trade" are actionable and industries need only show "adverse effects to trade" instead of injury to the entire Community industry within Europe. The Trade Barrier Regulation, therefore, is geared toward the problems encountered in entering third-country markets, much like Section 301. The real question is whether European countries and industries are any more likely to use the Trade Barrier Regulation for intellectual property disputes. Will bilateral dispute resolution flourish in Europe? Probably not. In order to build consensus among the member states, the commission, and the European Council, procedures remain complex and reaction times to trade practices abroad remain slow.

The European Commission is fully aware of the problem. Its new market access policy statements are reassuring to the United States in that they assert the need for full implementation of TRIPs and the desire to use bilateral mechanisms, including the withdrawal of benefits like General Systems of Preferences (GSP) when third countries do not fulfill their trade obligations.[99] Sir Leon Brittan, Vice-President of the European Commission, has been open about the need for the European Union to speak with one voice in trade matters. He has in fact lobbied to extend Article 113 of the Treaty of Rome—which gives the Commission authority in multilateral negotiations—to intellectual property rights, among other issues. His reasons are simple: finalizing international negotiations takes too much time because three unanimous approvals from the Council of Ministers are necessary; national legislatures then take two to three years to ratify trade agreements; unanimity means the European Union must adopt the lowest-common-denominator bargaining position, a fact exploited by other countries.[100]

In the absence of a large stick, Europe has focused its bilateral efforts on technical cooperation. Hard data on amounts spent are elusive, but Europe is thought to be one of the most important providers of technical assistance, both through the EU and through national programs.[101] The European Union will spend approxi-

---

[99] See European Commission, DG 1, "The Global Challenge of International Trade: A Market Access Strategy for the European Union," website— http://europa.eu.int/en/comm/dg01/feng.htm.

[100] From Lionel Barber, "Brussels Strives to Call the Tune on Trade," *Financial Times*, March 1996.

[101] Detailed descriptions of assistance programs are submitted by the advanced countries to the WTO in compliance with Article 67 of the TRIPs Agreement. Total expenditures on technical assistance are not published.

mately 4.5 million ECU on the IPR Cooperation Programme for China over five years, and a similar amount for technical cooperation in ASEAN countries. Since the European Commission has the power to extend technical aid, and to file complaints with the WTO, it has relied primarily on positive incentives and on retaliation within multilaterally sanctioned bounds to change the practices of third countries.

The main reason Europe is unlikely to use bilateral instruments to further its IP interests—and therefore unlikely to join the United States in the use of unilateral sanctions against third countries—is that it does not have the will to make those instruments effective and responsive to industry needs. In part this is due to the institutional tension of the European Commission and its relationship to the member states. But it is also due to differing interpretations of the necessity to press countries for ever higher IP standards.

The authority over intellectual property regulations is shared in the European Union by member states and the Commission. This "shared competency" has created a certain degree of tension, as countries are not always eager to give up sovereignty. In international forums, the European Commission is charged with coordinating member state positions in IP negotiations. It is itself a party to the WTO.[102] In bilateral negotiations with a third country, however, most believe that the Commission cannot initiate a complaint on its own—as the U.S. government can and regularly does—but must react to complaints from a member state or a company. Since the European Commission clearly can bring a case to the dispute settlement process within the WTO, it will probably prefer doing so over engaging in bilateral discussions that could be questioned by its own member states. The European Commission needs multilateral forums to sanction its involvement in IPR debates.

---

[102] The Commission was highly visible during the GATT TRIPs negotiations and at the WIPO New Instruments/Berne Protocol conference in December 1996.

The European Commission concern about market access, the need for proactive negotiation, and enforcement of trade rules is a relatively new orientation for Brussels.[103] The primary mission of the European Union has been to create a better business environment for Europeans within Europe, not to respond to extra-European private sector complaints. For this reason, there is no single body in the Commission with the ability and authority to flex European muscles in trade disputes. The USTR, by contrast, in the early 1970s formed the Advisory Committee on Trade Policy Negotiations (ACTPN), whose primary purpose is to alert the government to business concerns abroad. And while the office of the USTR is subject to the usual checks and balances, it has significant authority to make decisions about trade issues. This freedom is lacking in the Brussels bureaucracy.

Beyond these institutional factors, there has been a deep ideological divide between the United States and Europe in their approach to third countries. Europeans believe that while acceleration of TRIPs implementation is desirable, developing countries are entitled to the transition periods stipulated in the agreement. They do not believe that pressuring developing countries beyond what they bargained for is legitimate. In fact, during the TRIPs negotiations, the Europeans acted as moderator, softening the extreme positions of the United States on the one side and Brazil and India on the other.[104] Transition periods were the quid pro quo for uniform minimum standards of protection.

Moreover, Europe has frequently registered its distaste for American unilateral pressure tactics, embodied in Section 301, even though many Europeans privately acknowledge the usefulness of this approach and publicly the European Union has mim-

---

[103] In 1996 the Commission issued report entitled "A Market Access Strategy for the European Union," which outlines Europe's new orientation.

[104] In part, this may be because Spain, Portugal, Greece, and Italy were reluctant to adopt some sections of the TRIPs Agreement themselves.

icked it in the Trade Barrier Regulation. Americans argue that the aggressive U.S. approach has been a boon to European negotiators because they can enter the fray after the United States has, thanks to the threat of retaliation, and forge their own bilateral agreement. The tactic looks suspiciously like free-riding, given that the Europeans did not waste any political clout for changing the third country's IP behavior. From the European perspective, however, Section 301 makes cooperation infeasible. Since the European Union has itself frequently been the target of Section 301 investigations, it cannot lend support to a measure it decries as unfair and extralegal when used against Europe. The preferred EU approach, therefore, for changing behavior behind borders is the donation of technical aid. Internationally sanctioned retaliation, however, is okay by Europe. It is willing to file WTO complaints—as it did against Japan's sound-recording copyright laws and against India and Pakistan for their failure to set up a mailbox system for filing patent applications as stipulated in the TRIPs Agreement.

The WTO's Dispute Settlement Body holds out the promise that Europe will become more proactive in its policies toward third countries, as the EU does not have ideological objections to using this multilaterally sanctioned forum. It is unlikely, however, that Europe will single out a WTO member for TRIPs-plus implementation because of its greater tolerance for the transition periods. There is a slightly greater, though still slim, possibility that Europe might start a Trade Regulation Barrier case against a non-WTO member. Given the ideological divide, the United States cannot expect Europe to be a kindred spirit in its use of bilateral trade pressure, especially not in Asia, where Europe's influence is weak.

Cooperating with Japan

Japan has even fewer bilateral tools at its immediate disposal to direct against its trade partners, and it has a similar distrust of unilateral sanctions. Like Europe, Japan would prefer to bring IP disputes into a multilateral context, but it is even less proactive on the matter of shaping global IP regimes. Most telling, Japan has not yet initiated any complaints in the WTO pertaining to intellectual property violations. Based on past behavior, the United States can assume that Japan is unlikely to be a staunch ally of aggressive American IP tactics.

Japan is not at the helm of an all-Asian trade organization that would allow it a greater voice in the formulation of regional trade policies. In fact, the United States has actively discouraged the formation of any such group.[105] Japan has, however, been active in APEC, taking the lead in an initiative to make Asia's intellectual property regulations more transparent and discussions about how to enhance protection in trademarks and standardize patent filings.[106] So far the APEC meetings have not yielded any regional standards for IP protection, and if any are reached in the near future, they are expected to represent conservative improvements on TRIPs.

Japan is uninterested in playing power politics in intellectual property rights. During the American showdown with China, for example, Japan maintained official neutrality, privately advising that economic engagement—rather than threats of trade sanctions—is the best way to bring the PRC into the international system.[107] Country specialists explain that Japan does not like to use confrontational tactics, and that its government believes that eco-

---

[105] Joseph M. Grieco makes this point in "Realism and Regionalism: American Power and German and Japanese Institutional Strategies during and after the Cold War," paper presented at the annual meeting of the American Political Science Association, August 29-September 1, 1996.

[106] APEC's 1996 Collective Action Agenda included several agreements to further discussions on IPR.

[107] Christopher Johnstone, "Tokyo Reticent as U.S.-China Trade War Looms," *Japan Economic Indicators Report*, no. 20B, pp. 5–6, May 24, 1996.

nomic development is the fastest route to a strong IP regime.[108] To that end, the Japanese provide technical expertise and financial support to establish new administrative and judicial branches needed for the IP systems of developing countries in Asia.[109]

It is also important to remember that Japan is, and thinks of itself as, an exporting nation. Japan has had annual export surpluses above $100 billion through the 1990s.[110] In 1995 Japan's surplus with Asia alone totaled $70 billion. And although Japan is importing more from Asia than in the past, over the course of the decade its surplus with Asia has grown more than 20 percent a year. The products exported are primarily machinery, and transportation equipment, while its imports have a lesser IP component (major import sectors include food, raw materials, fuels, manufactured goods, machinery, and transport equipment).[111] Because Japan imports few technically sophisticated products and has no problem exporting to its neighbors, the government is unconvinced that it would be worthwhile to pressure trade partners for stronger IP protection. While individual Japanese companies do complain about piracy, the United States should not expect Japan

---

[108] The Japanese and the American systems of IP protection are substantially different, and have been the cause of many trade disputes. The United States would probably object were Japan to exercise a heavy hand in forming the IP systems of other Asian countries. For a discussion of the major U.S.-Japanese differences, see Koichi Hamada, "Protection of Intellectual Property Rights in Japan," Economic Growth Center at Yale University, April 1996.

[109] Koichi Hamada, "Protection of Intellectual Property Rights in Japan."

[110] In 1995 the Japanese trade surplus was $135 billion and the American trade deficit was $158 billion.

[111] Seventy percent of total exports from Japan were machinery and transportation equipment. The figures in this paragraph are from the Japanese Ministry of Finance and the U.S. Department of Commerce as published in Japan Economic Institute, "Statistical Profile, International Transactions of Japan and the United States in 1995," *JEI Report* no. 34A, September 13, 1996.

to be a reliable or independent supporter of strong IP standards in Asia.[112]

Instead, Japan's strategy in IPRs has been to provide technical expertise and financial support to build administrative and judicial branches in developing countries. In 1996 Japan doubled its contribution to the WIPO secretariat for technical training in Asia. It also cooperates bilaterally with Asian countries that request aid. The United States believes that enforcing IP rights is simply a matter of will. The Japanese believe it is futile to force countries to adopt strong IP regimes until they are economically developed.

Limited Resources

Limited resources—both monetary and political—are the second set of constraints on American IP policymaking. Financially, the costs of raising IP standards worldwide will put a burden on many developing countries. Two types of costs need to be considered: (1) costs to industry associated with increased licensing payments, and (2) costs to governments associated with setting up a modern IPR system. By one measure, the costs of increased royalty and licensing payments by the South to the North could "double or triple the foreign exchange outflow caused by Third World annual debt payments."[113] To offset the potential technological isolation of developing countries that will not be able to pay for technology, APEC and the WTO have pledged to increase technology transfer from developed to developing nations (although the types of pro-

---

[112] And given many disagreements with Japan over IP issues, the U.S. may not welcome a forceful Japanese presence in international IP negotiations. For a good overview of disagreements about IP protection for software, see Joel West, "Software Rights and Japan's Shift to an Information Society," *Asian Survey*, vol. 35, no. 12 (December 1995), pp. 1118–39.

[113] Figures from the Rural Advancement Fund International, quoted in de Almeida, "The Political Economy of Intellectual Property Protection: Technological Protectionism and the Transfer of Revenue among Nations," *International Journal of Technology Management*, vol. 10, no. 2/3 (1995), pp. 214–29..

grams this will entail and how they will be paid for remains unclear).[114]

Of more immediate concern to the United States is the behind-the-border implementation of intellectual property regulations. Monitoring and implementation is expected to be more expensive than enacting the legal foundations of an IP regime, but costs will vary widely. Laos and Cambodia would have to create IP regimes essentially from scratch, while Argentina and Brazil only have to tinker with systems that already have relatively high standards. For many developing countries, a lack of funding and expertise means that governments may not be capable of establishing in a timely fashion the administrative and legal structures—not to mention the legal culture—that must underpin any IP system. Technical assistance and financial aid is necessary to upgrade these IP regimes.

The actual costs to each country are hard to estimate, and depend on the route each country chooses.[115] The United States aids developing countries through visiting scholar training programs, conferences, and consultations with foreign governments on how to set up or improve their patent, trademark, and copyright systems and how to fulfill TRIPs obligations. The most visible agency abroad is the USTR, but it is a trade negotiator, not an intellectual property rights enforcer. However, the Patent and

---

[114] Article 67 of the TRIPs agreement stipulates that developed countries shall provide technical and financial assistance to developing countries. In APEC, the Osaka Action Agenda of 1995 also included a clause on the need for technical assistance and technology transfer to reduce disparities in economic development.

[115] For example, many countries choose to charge fees for filing patents and trademarks in order to cover the costs of administering the IP system (however, fees usually do not cover new expenses incurred by the judicial system and customs services). In addition, since establishing a patent system with the independent capacity to search for prior art and evaluate patents in every country would be very expensive, WIPO suggests that developing countries rely on the search and examination decisions of one of the advanced developed countries (e.g., the U.S. Patent and Trade Office, the Japan Patent Office, or the European Patent Office) to minimize patent-related expenses.

Trademark Office, the Justice Department, the Commerce Department, the U.S. Information Agency, and the U.S. Agency for International Development (USAID) are involved in aid and technical assistance programs. Continued funding of these programs is critical if the United States wants strong IP systems to emerge worldwide.

The World Intellectual Property Organization is by far the biggest source of advice, training, and documentation for developing countries. With its $200 million budget financed primarily through fees, it costs the U.S. government relatively little. In addition, the private sector plays an important role in educating developing countries. Groups like the Business Software Alliance, the Pharmaceutical Manufacturers and Researchers of America, and the International Intellectual Property Association spend a good deal of time abroad providing information and training on how to abide by the TRIPs Agreement and explaining the benefits of doing so. And promises of investment by foreign companies can also go a long way in changing practices.

To a certain extent, the United States can expect outside funding to be available for developing countries. Japan is enthusiastic about sponsoring IP seminars to train officials in East Asia, and the European Union is also well funded for technical assistance in IP. [116]

The United States privately hopes that these countries will continue their activities, although aware that foreign models of IP protection—Japan's in particular—are not always in harmony with the American one. Nevertheless, if the United States is to shape global IP regimes, it should think of foreign governments and the private sector as supplements to, not substitutes for, U.S. assistance to countries building modern intellectual property systems.

---

[116] Koichi Hamada, "Protection of Intellectual Property Rights in Japan."

Narrow Negotiating Margins

Beyond the isolation of U.S. policies and the uncertain funding to follow up trade agreements, conflicting political goals hinder a coherent IP policy. To raise standards further, the United States needs to wield credible threats or to dole out attractive benefits in exchange for cooperation. Unfortunately, the negotiating tools at its disposal are no longer as effective as in the past, and paying for stronger rights is an expensive strategy. The United States has less and less leverage when it acts alone to influence the IP behavior of its trade partners. Countries know that American threats of unilateral sanctions are rarely carried out, and can be challenged within the WTO.[117] Benefits offered to developing countries, like GSP, are outside the purview of the WTO and can still be used to exact changes, but as average U.S. tariff levels fall, the marginal damage incurred by developing countries from the withdrawal of GSP privileges becomes less threatening. [118]

Moreover, from a purely diplomatic perspective, the United States can only cash in its chips so many times. Intellectual property issues will sometimes take a back seat to other trade or foreign policy priorities. In politically fragile countries caution and patience is necessary, as pushing too hard a line on intellectual property may backfire. And in countries with the geostrategic importance of China or Russia, the United States is unlikely to incite

---

[117] In 1988 Brazil threatened to take the United States to the GATT if it did not drop its proposed Section 301 sanctions. The United States backed off.

[118] The GSP is the Generalized System of Preferences. Also relevant are the Caribbean Basin Initiative and the Andean Trade Preferences Act.

a trade war over intellectual property since so many other security or economic interests hang in the balance.

The intellectual property battles the United States pursues in the future must be particularly well chosen because it will fight them alone, it will fight them without deep pockets, and such battles will require more patience and commitment than in the past. These constraints limit the strategies open to the United States.

THE ASIA CHALLENGE

TO RECAP, THE DEEP American concern with intellectual property infringement is a product of the dramatic political and economic shifts in trade during the past two decades. The United States cares about piracy because the damage inflicted by intellectual property infringement hits America's fast-growing and information-intensive industries hardest. While pirates are active globally, Asia is the Bermuda Triangle of IP. Since Asia is less dependent on U.S. markets than Latin America, the United States cannot easily put a stop to infringement there. Complicating matters further, American concern has shifted since the TRIPs Agreement from simply negotiating IP agreements to monitoring and enforcing them behind borders, which is a much more difficult task requiring time to build native support. Ideally, the United States could collaborate with Europe and Japan in rapidly raising international IP rights to a uniform standard and underwriting the implementation process, but in reality coordination among the advanced industrialized countries is spotty. How then should the United States approach the big emerging markets in Asia?

So far the United States has used a cocktail of unilateral, plurilateral, and multilateral mechanisms—none of which it plans to give up. At present, the temptation may be to lean on bilateral negotiations. Indeed, the United States recently concluded a bilateral copyright agreement with Vietnam. Such bilateral discussions with foreign countries about their IP practices are useful, but for a number of reasons unilateral pressure should be yielded to only infrequently. First, bilateralism can backfire, and Asia particularly resents and resists unilateral pressure for stronger intellectual property rights because its use seems arbitrary and its benefits uncertain. Second, the latitude for unilateral action is increasingly circumscribed, both by the WTO and by the ability of the United States to retaliate effectively against countries. Third, the stigma attached to being cited by the USTR for poor IP practices is dependent on the credibility of our threats, and on the negative signal sent to investors. Overused unilateral pressure lessens both its threat and its effectiveness as an investment flag. Finally, bilateral agreements work against the long-term goal of creating global standards in intellectual property protection. They lead, rather, to a patchwork of uneven IP protection.

Bilateral agreements are most attractive when prospects for progress elsewhere are not good. Indeed, at the moment no large-scale multilateral negotiations are imminent, and future WTO rounds are expected to focus on new issues of competition policy, including labor standards and procurement policies. The TRIPs Agreement was not center stage in the December 1996 Ministerial Meeting, and intellectual property may remain a dormant issue until full review of implementation is over in the year 2000. But in Asia there are good alternative forums for IP negotiations in the APEC and ASEAN regional groupings, which should prevent the United States from resorting automatically to unilateralism.

Regional Agreements

Regional trade agreements are a good alternative to multilateral negotiations because they too allow cross-issue bargaining between countries. For example, to entice developing countries to go beyond their TRIPs commitments, the United States can offer collateral concessions, such as aid for establishing the IP infrastructure, allowing some compulsory licensing, or otherwise facilitating access to the U.S. market. The participation of several countries—and especially several developed countries—endows regional trade agreements with greater weight and authority than bilateral agreements. Regional agreements even have an advantage over multilateralism, in that the smaller number of countries involved can reach higher levels of standardization than can GATT or WIPO because participating nations are more likely to share some goals and the payoffs can be more targeted.

The combination of strength and flexibility in regional trade arrangements has spawned an impressive number of groupings, most of which are negotiating intellectual property agreements. The list includes NAFTA, MERCOSUR, the Free Trade Area of the Americas, APEC, the ASEAN, and, among the advanced industrialized countries, the Transatlantic Dialogue and the EU. [119] Many of these are relatively young organizations. Their self-declared interest in pursuing intellectual property issues is testament to the growing consciousness of the importance of IP for innovation and trade.

APEC in particular represents one of the United States's greatest opportunities for extending its IP policies regionally. The 18 APEC countries, centered in Asia, are committed to accelerating the implementation of the Uruguay Round and to broadening and deepening its accomplishments.[120] In the summer of 1996, the APEC Collective Action Agenda included seven intellectual property stipulations. Countries have agreed to (1) meet more frequently to discuss IP issues of common concern; (2) compile a survey of national IP laws; (3) create IP contact and enforcement lists to facilitate communication; (4) explore enhanced protection for trademarks regionally; (5) discuss simplification and stan-

---

[119] MERCOSUR adopted a common protocol for trademarks in 1995, and discussions on copyrights are underway. See Robert M. Sherwood and Carlos A. Primo Braga, "Intellectual Property, Trade and Economic Development: A Road Map for FTAA Negotiations," unpublished paper, 1996. The Free Trade Association of the Americas groups 34 countries in the hemisphere and hopes to create a free-trade area by 2005. Although IPRs are under discussion, no agreement has yet been reached. In an effort to improve Asia's IPRs, the member countries of ASEAN recently have agreed to create a single patent and trademark agency (similar in concept to the EPO) to enforce intellectual property rights in the region.

[120] See "APEC Economic Leaders' Declaration of Common Resolve," Osaka, Japan, November 1995. website—http://www.apecsec.org.sg/osaka.html.

dardization of Asian-Pacific patent filing; (6) review enforcement problems; and (7) explore high-level, or TRIPs-plus, IP protection.

APEC offers other U.S. trade initiatives, offering an alternative, nonconfrontational venue for venting trade concerns. As a cooperative forum, its meetings work to accelerate the evolution of IP by familiarizing countries with the advantages of stronger IPRs. There is even a degree of competition between countries to appear serious about their commitment to APEC, and stronger IP rights, which also accelerates reform. In APEC the United States can join forces with Japan, and even the newly industrialized economies, to gain leverage in IP discussions. These countries generate a great deal of intellectual property themselves, and would benefit from IP standards. Strength in numbers is necessary to gradually upgrade intellectual property protection, as the Pacific is home to many countries—China, Indonesia, and the Philippines, for instance—that have continuously defied U.S. unilateral efforts. Finally, APEC creates a framework for offering positive incentives. Already the United States and Japan help educate lawyers, judges, and government functionaries in the region who are to administer national IP systems, and discussions have started on building regional information centers and perhaps, eventually, regional registries.

But the allure of APEC is mitigated by its unusual framework. Unlike in a traditional free-trade area, initiatives are self-driven or episodic. Each country identifies its own "Individual Action Plan" for liberalization. Within this framework each country sets "soft" voluntary targets with the aim of completely opening trade by 2010 for the advanced countries and 2020 for the developing countries. But progress on this formal path has been slow. So far the greatest achievements have come from APEC's episodic identification of sectors suitable for a big liberalization push in the WTO, notably information technology goods and telecom services (both at the Subic summit in 1996). However, there is no formal cross-sector linkage (for example, textile liberalization in exchange for stronger IP rights), and this detracts from APEC's role as a regional agreement where IP agreements might be negotiated.[121]

In this environment, Japan is comfortable with taking an educational approach to changing the IP behavior of its neighbors. A cautious, incentive-oriented strategy is well suited to APEC's novel structure and its politically and economically diverse membership. APEC is unlikely to enact concrete and binding measures, such as the expansion of product category coverage or the resolution of how to treat parallel imports, and progress is likely to be slow. No formal decisions on regional standards for IP protection have been made, and if any are reached they are expected to be conservative improvements on TRIPs.

Thus the United States finds itself in a bind in APEC. On one hand, the United States has IP disputes with almost all the member countries that it would like to address directly. But despite the enormity of IP challenges in Asia, APEC is not organizationally capable of a radical renegotiation of TRIPs commitments.[122] While APEC is unlikely to forge a stronger IP agreement than that under the Uruguay Round anytime soon, it allows the United States to engage several big emerging markets, China in particular, in discussions about global IP protection. The value of these positive measures should not be underestimated, as ultimately IPRs will have meaning only if there are domestic interest groups that are committed to their enforcement.

---

[121] The APEC guiding principles do include comprehensive coverage of all sectors may allow for some inter-sector discussions.

[122] Some of the smaller regional groupings, like ASEAN, hold greater promise of pushing Asia forward with their plans of coordinating patent and trademark laws and creating joint institutions.

Cooperation Among Advanced Countries

An agreement among advanced industrialized countries that coordinates IP policies toward the developing world would also serve to spur changes in Asia. A unified approach to third countries increases bargaining power in multilateral forums and reduces the creation of divergent regional IP trajectories, always a danger in pursuing multiple regional IP strategies. In addition, many international IP issues remain unresolved and could benefit from partial resolution among the developed nations. Examples of such issues include some divergent interpretations of the TRIPs agreement; how countries deal with new technologies like global information networks and biotechnology; and how to rationalize and harmonize national administrative procedures for granting intellectual property rights.[123] By reaching consensus on these thorny issues, the North could pave the way for their broader acceptance in the WTO or WIPO.[124]

The United States and Europe have been flirting with the notion of a transatlantic agreement to revive a flagging economic and security relationship.[125] At the Madrid summit of December 1995, proposals for intellectual property cooperation recommended the identification of "specific areas of desired action" and "common positions leading towards the improvement of IPR protection

---

[123] Disagreement in TRIPs exist over the interpretation of when intellectual property rights are "exhausted" and what type of compulsory licensing is permitted. Improvements might include a reduction in the cost of European filing, converting the U.S. system to a first-to-file system, and harmonizing publication grace periods and opposition rules.

[124] For an elaboration of the importance of coordinating policy and the difficulties of doing so, see Richard Steinberg, "Transatlantic Management of the Global Trading System," in Bruce Stokes, ed., *Open for Business: Creating a Transatlantic Marketplace,* New York: Council on Foreign Relations, 1996, pp. 97–112.

[125] For a discussion of the format, content, and likelihood of a transatlantic free trade area, see Bruce Stokes, ed., *Open For Business*, New York: Council on Foreign Relations, 1995.

[73]

within and outside the reach of the WTO and WIPO."[126] The Transatlantic Business Dialogue (TABD) stated a need for rapid and full implementation of the TRIPs agreement worldwide, for EU-U.S. cooperation to monitor compliance, and for the creation of a joint strategy for IP by the first full review of the WTO in 1999-2000. These dates are far more important than can be hoped for from APEC or NAFTA for the refinement and deepening of global IP commitments. While the EU-U.S. discussions are significant, they represent the first, tentative steps toward the creation of a new transatlantic agenda. Perhaps its greatest benefit is as a discussion forum for industries in which both sides of the Atlantic can explore parallel interests in IP. In the near term, however, one cannot expect a formal agreement to cooperate on third-country IP policy.

Nevertheless, a more united front on IPRs—especially one that included Japan—would smooth relations between advanced countries, minimize divergence among free-trade areas, and help move forward future multilateral agreements.

Beyond Regionalism

Regional agreements represent one strategy for furthering IP standards, but they cannot be the only tool. Many countries fall outside the regional nets, including giants like India and Russia. India is especially problematic, challenging patent decisions for pharmaceutical and agricultural products. Unilateral pressure may not be capable of pushing India to adopt and enforce a higher level of IP protection, given that its reliance on the U.S. market, which was never huge, is now diminishing.

Ultimately the U.S. goal is to set up a rules-based multilateral system that includes the largest number of countries possible. A

---

[126] Many of the proposals were culled from the suggestions of a group of 100 American and European business representatives called the Transatlantic Business Dialogue. See the TABD Progress Report, May 23, 1996. Internet site— http://iepnt1.itaiep.doc.gov/tabd/progress.htm.

seamless intellectual property protection system, in which national boundaries do not matter, is a long-term objective, but strong global standards are more immediately achievable. Regional agreements are good for creating consensus and raising standards locally, but they must be woven together into a consistent multilateral system that is easy to monitor and administer. In its dealings with Asia, therefore, the United States must keep its eye on the global prize. The WTO and WIPO remain important players.

The most important, and least tested, aspect of the WTO is its improved dispute settlement mechanism, which, ideally, is to be an alternative to unilateral pressure in trade disputes.[127] In the new systems, quasijudicial panels have been strengthened allowing no single country to veto an adverse ruling. Countries found at fault will be required to comply with dispute settlement panel rulings, or the aggrieved party will be allowed to retaliate. Historical precedent in GATT suggests that when a defendant is found in violation, nearly 90 per cent of the cases result in full or partial satisfaction of the claim.[128] Of the 20 cases the United States had filed with the WTO by the end of 1996, it has lost none and won one. The remaining 18 were settled outside the WTO, largely to the satisfaction of the United States.

---

[127] For a discussion of dispute settlement in GATT and the WTO, who uses the system and who gains from it, see Christina Sevilla, "Complaints and Compliance: The Politics of Enforcing GATT/WTO Rules," unpublished paper delivered at the Annual Meeting of the American Political Science Association, San Francisco, 1996.

[128] Ibid.

Table 4. IPR dispute settlement cases initiated or planned by the United States at the WTO

		Resolution
Japan	1996	preexisting sound recordings, issue resolved
Portugal	1996	patent term, issue resolved
Pakistan	1996	"mailbox system," issue resolved
India	1996	"mailbox system," dispute to appear before WTO panel
Turkey	1996	foreign firm tax, in negotiation
Indonesia	1996	trademarks, in negotiation
Denmark	1997	enforcement issue, U.S. plans to initiate WTO case
Sweden	1997	enforcement issue, U.S. plans to initiate WTO case
Ireland	1997	copyright laws, U.S. plans to initiate WTO case
Ecuador	1997	general TRIPs obligation, US plans to initiate WTO case

The United States has had a very positive experience with the WTO dispute system in intellectual property. Of the six IP cases filed by early 1997 three were resolved bilaterally without the use of a WTO dispute panel. Japan has agreed to extend copyright protection to sound recordings made before 1971. Portugal has agreed to bring its patent laws into TRIPs compliance. Pakistan set up the required mailbox system for pharmaceutical and agrochemical patent applications. Two cases have not yet been resolved. Negotiations with Indonesia about discriminatory trademark protection and with Turkey about its box office tax on foreign films continue, but no panel has been set up. (The latter is, strictly speaking, a market access issue, but it affects a copyright-dependent industry.) Only the Indian mailbox case is at an impasse and will be heard by a WTO panel. The Indian government has not set up the required filing system, despite repeated assurances to the United States that it would do so. On the whole, the WTO dispute settlement system is proving useful to the United States. Plans to initiate four, and possibly six, new cases were announced in May 1997.

The dispute settlement mechanism is the pièce de résistance in TRIPs, promising developed and developing countries a chance to be complainants in IP disputes, to receive redress, and to shape the international IP system.[129] To take full advantage of the dispute settlement mechanism, the United States has set up an agreements and compliance center within the Department of Commerce to monitor compliance with trade agreements abroad, and the EU is considering a similar body. The more information one has on compliance, the easier it is to lodge complaints. Unlike in GATT, which turned a blind eye to their violations by developing countries, LDCs are being brought fully into the WTO trading system and must comply with all the commitments and notifications required of members. Four of the six initial IP cases were against developing countries.

But at the same time, developing countries have gained the ability to become complainants themselves. Most trade complaints in GATT and the WTO have been lodged against developed countries by other developed countries. With the WTO, however, there has been a rise in complaints by less-developed countries, both among themselves and against the United States and the EC.[130] Therefore, from the point of view of less-developed countries, the WTO may be more attractive than a regional forum for future IP negotiations with the United States. The WTO reduces

---

[129] Sevilla, "Complaints and Compliance: The Politics of Enforcing GATT/WTO Rules."

[130] Ibid.

the American use of unilateral pressure to force change, and the dispute settlement procedure devolves power to aggrieved parties, regardless of size.

Regional agreements in Asia should be understood, therefore, as an addition to, not a replacement for, the WTO. Of course, APEC needs to be WTO-legal, but the United States must in addition try to use the WTO as much as possible. Its dispute settlement mechanism may prove invaluable in resolving global IP disputes (as in the recent cases against Japan, Pakistan, and Portugal). If the resolution of future cases proves satisfactory, the WTO will be a great back-up, maintaining minimum levels of protection in countries where the United States cannot engage in bilateral or regional negotiations. Finally, the WTO and WIPO remain necessary to slowly bring up standards in developing countries to which the United States cannot devote its limited resources. The United States must continue to pursue IP disputes within the multilateral forums because of their ability to bring a large number of countries together to create, and abide by, new rules of the road for international trade.

CONCLUSIONS

OVER THE PAST ten years, the world's understanding of intellectual property has radically evolved. Once an inviolable element of national technology policy, intellectual property rights are now an international trade concern. IPRs are no longer anathema to developing countries, and advanced nations are switching their focus to behind-the-border monitoring and compliance with agreements. These are impressive changes, despite the many loopholes that trouble American IP developers.

Strangely, U.S. policy has not evolved as rapidly. The USTR's approach to weak intellectual property rights abroad remains grounded in the concerns and rhetoric of the mid-1980s. In fact, it is difficult to distinguish Clinton's IP policy from that of Bush or even Reagan. USTR officials are quick to point out the continuity, despite the creation of the WTO, in the U.S. multitrack approach to IP negotiations. But the tools presently available to the United States feel dull or inappropriate for the fine task of monitoring behind-the-border compliance and creating domestic constituencies that will autonomously clamor for IP protection. New strategies are necessary to meet novel challenges.

In its second term, the Clinton administration has a unique opportunity to remodel American IP practices. The timing is perfect. The WTO is new and relatively untested; Clinton is a lame-duck president with a certain freedom to rework trade policies; and the next few years are critical for engaging developing countries in further IP negotiations. The challenge is to stop making intellectual property a divisive issue, and to create a consistent, transparent policy that will inspire confidence in and a commitment to intellectual property protection in the big emerging markets.

There are several improvements the Clinton administration should consider. First, the United States would benefit by articulating a two-track approach to TRIPs. On one hand, the creation of a smooth international intellectual property system demands that the United States put its full support behind the TRIPs agreement. On the other hand, the United States can and should use its leverage to accelerate TRIPs implementation with a handful of specifically identified big emerging markets. Bifurcating U.S. goals will foster greater confidence in the international IP system while still moving the standardization process forward.

Full support of the TRIPs Agreement entails not only bringing violations to the WTO's Dispute Settlement Body but permitting many developing and all the least developed countries to use their allotted grace periods for fulfilling TRIPs commitments. Despite being a signatory to TRIPs, implicit in the present U.S. strategy is pressure on a disparate group of developing countries to accelerate implementation. In other words, while the United States signed the TRIPs agreement, it wants TRIPs-plus implementation. But since the United States can only employ bilateral measures when the rest of its trade relationship with a partner is solid or when it has little to lose, not all countries are subject to equal scrutiny. This impatience lends a schizophrenic or opportunistic tone to the American use of bilateralism.

In contrast, the benefits of the WTO are precisely its consistency and broad base. By honoring the TRIPs timeline (while closely monitoring its implementation), the United States would signal that its first priority is the creation of a *global* system of protection. A strong multilateral forum for IP is important if it is to reach a large number of countries, establish minimum levels of protection, and resolve IP disputes. The WTO and WIPO can reach and aid the small and medium-size countries that the United States, Europe, and Japan do not have the resources to actively target. But the value of the WTO and WIPO is much greater, as forums trusted by the developed and developing nations for future negotiations on intellectual property.

That said, the Clinton administration should explicitly acknowledge its desire to accelerate TRIPs implementation through regional agreements with the large and dynamic developing countries. Specifically, the United States can and should set higher goals for the richer developing countries of the Western Hemisphere (for instance, Chile, Argentina, and Brazil) and possibly the Pacific. The bifurcated strategy requires that the United States explicitly identify TRIPs-plus candidates, and articulate why they should be subject to advanced-country norms.

For example, NAFTA allows the United States to dictate to future members that accession is premised on strong IPRs. The potential for NAFTA expansion has already had a ripple effect throughout Latin America, an advantage the United States should exploit. APEC may be harder to influence. Certainly the new enthusiasm for regional trade organizations works in favor of the United States because many of the groups are actively harmonizing IP standards and creating regional patent and trademark offices (as ASEAN is planning to do). To create a global IP protection system, the United States should encourage all such regional efforts, including APEC. But discussions in APEC may fail to reach TRIPs-plus goals, and the United States should be ready to accept that as long as the countries fully abide by the TRIPs Agreement. China, Thailand, Indonesia, and India will need time to create legal systems capable of enforcing stronger IP regulations. APEC will be important in creating a support structure and minimizing costs. It may not substantially accelerate the process, however.

A second improvement in the Clinton IP strategy would be a clear and unified policy of financial and technical aid for developing countries that are revamping the judicial, customs, and administrative structures underpinning intellectual property—especially for countries identified as TRIPs-plus candidates. Presently the United States has an ad hoc system of technical and financial aid that does not match funding problem piracy with regions. The United States should systematically gather information on IP practices, abuses, and costs. Better estimates of losses due to piracy, by country and by product category, would help identify problem areas. In addition, greater information about the effect of stronger IP rights on investment, technology transfer, job creation, and innovativeness in developing countries—especially evaluations by economists from less-developed countries—would help in convincing countries that the economic payoffs are worth the political risks. The work should be fascinating; natural laboratories like Mexico and Brazil furnish goldmines of information for empirical research. Such an IP information policy could be coordinated multilaterally, through WIPO or the WTO.

A third improvement would be to involve Europe and Japan in IP policymaking more fully. The United States definitely plays the "bad cop" to European and Japanese "good cops" in intellectual property negotiations. The confluence of Northern interests in stronger IP rights should allow for a more united front against the most egregious IP pirates. A triangulation of strategies, or at least a commitment to emphasize the importance of IP to each region, would facilitate the task of raising standards enormously either through bilateral negotiation and pressure or through multilateral organizations.

Finally, the United States needs to resolve the place of IP in trade policy. While it is true that the some of the most advanced high-technology and export-intensive sectors suffer from piracy, the sectors in question are limited and their losses relatively sustainable. These industries should influence, but not dictate, the U.S. position on IP policy. In fact, a broader public debate recently erupted over the protection of digital information and databases. Through this debate, the interests of the print, music, and video industries in controlling digital works are being balanced against those of Internet users, Internet companies, libraries, and scientists who want to maintain affordable access to Internet information sources. In general, wrangling over the desired balance in IP policy is necessary to prevent its capture by limited interest groups.

Conclusions

The government must also remember that intellectual property policy is not a magic bullet. Strong and global IPRs will not automatically spur development or ensure that corporations succeed in new markets. The rationale for protection is primarily to encourage investment in creative research and artistic works, at home and abroad. Since IP is but one part of a country's economic problems, countries should not hang their hopes or fears on IP policies alone. American IP policies, therefore, must be part of a larger trade strategy. Since funding and the political stamina for IP battles are not limitless, U.S. IP policy should dovetail with its larger goals in Asia and elsewhere.

There is probably no single best IP strategy to achieve American goals because both the global trading system and what constitutes intellectual property are moving targets. But American interests have changed remarkably since Trollope's time and even since the end of the Uruguay Round. U.S. IP policies must also evolve to create a sustainable discussion on standards with developing countries, in a forum that does not force us to create unnecessary trade conflicts. Part of such a strategy requires bilateralism to be de-emphasized in favor of more active regional and multilateral strategies.

BIBLIOGRAPHY

Alford, William P. *To Steal a Book Is an Elegant Offense: Intellectual Property Law in Chinese Civilization*, Stanford, Calif.: Stanford University Press, 1995.

"APEC Economic Leaders' Declaration of Common Resolve." Osaka, Japan, November 1995. Internet site—http://www.a pecsec.org. sg/osaka. html.

Bale, Harvey E., Jr. "External Pressure: Does it Work? The Case of Pharmaceuticals." Unpublished paper for the Council on Foreign Relations study group American IPR Policy after the TRIPs Agreement. Washington, D.C., June 6, 1996.

Barton, John H. "Adapting the Intellectual Property System to New Technologies." In National Research Council, *Global Dimensions of Intellectual Property Rights in Science and Technology*. Washington, D.C.: National Academy Press, 1993.

Bayard, Thomas O., and Kimberly Ann Elliot. *Reciprocity and Retaliation in US Trade Policy*. Washington, D.C.: Institute for International Economics, 1994.

Correa, Carlos M. "Intellectual Property Rights and Foreign Direct Investment." *International Journal of Technology Management,* 10, no. 2/3 (1995), pp. 173–99.

de Almeida, Paulo R. "The Political Economy of Intellectual Property Protection: Technological Protectionism and the Transfer of Revenue among Nations." *International Journal of Technology Management,* 10, no. 2/3 (1995), pp. 214–29.

Destler, I.M. *American Trade Politics*. Washington, D.C.: Institute for International Economics, 1995.

Bibliography

Ellis, William T. "Patent and Copyright Protection for Software in the Post-TRIPs World." Unpublished paper for the Council on Foreign Relations study group, American IPR Policy after the TRIPs Agreement, March 1996.

Garten, Jeffrey. "The Big Emerging Markets." *Columbia Journal of World Business* 31, no. 2 (Summer 1996), pp. 6–31.

Gorlin, Jacques J. "U.S. Intellectual Property Policy After TRIPS." Unpublished paper for the Council on Foreign Relations study group American IPR Policy after the TRIPs Agreement, June 1996.

Grieco, Joseph M. "Realism and Regionalism: American Power and German and Japanese Institutional Strategies during and after the Cold War." Paper presented at the annual meeting of the American Political Science Association, August 29-September 1, 1996.

Hamada, Koichi. "Protection of Intellectual Property Rights in Japan." Unpublished paper presented to the Council on Foreign Relations study group American IPR Policy after the TRIPs Agreement, April 1996.

Icaza, Antonio Medina Mora. "The Mexican Software Industry." In The National Research Council's *Global Dimensions of Intellectual Property Rights in Science and Technology*. Washington, D.C.: National Academy Press, 1992.

International Intellectual Property Alliance. "IIPA Names 29 Countries Causing over $6 Billion in Trade Losses." Washington, D.C.: *International Intellectual Property Alliance,* February 20, 1996.

IMF. *International Financial Statistics Yearbook*, Washington, D.C., 1994.

Industry Functional Advisory Committee on Intellectual Property Rights. "Report to the Congress on the Uruguay Round," January 10, 1994.

Pirates on the High Seas

Japan Economic Institute. "Statistical Profile, International Transactions of Japan and the United States in 1995." *Japan Economic Institute Report,* no. 34A (September 13, 1996).

Johnstone, Christopher. "Tokyo Reticent as U.S.-China Trade War Looms." *Japan Economic Indicators Report* no. 20B (May 24, 1996), pp. 5–6.

Kahler, Miles. "International Institutions and the Political Economy of Integration." In *Integrating National Economies*. Washington, D.C.: The Brookings Institution, 1995.

Krugman, Paul, ed. *Strategic Trade Policy and the New International Economics*. Cambridge, Mass.: MIT Press, 1986.

Lannert, John, "Latin Notas," *Billboard*, February 24, 1996.

Mansfield, Edwin. "Intellectual Property Protection, Foreign Direct Investment, and Technology Transfer." Discussion Paper 19. Washington, D.C.: International Finance Corporation, 1994.

Maskus, Keith. "Regionalism and the Protection of IPRs." Unpublished paper presented to the Council on Foreign Relations study group, American IPR Policy after the TRIPs Agreement. May 22, 1996.

Moshavi, Sharon. "Bollywood Breaks into the Big Time." *Business Week* September 25, 1995, pp. 122–23.

Murashige, Kate H. "Industrial Policy and Biotechnology—Can Intellectual Property Protection Systems Catch Up?" Unpublished paper presented to the Council on Foreign Relations study group American IPR Policy after the TRIPs Agreement, March 1996.

National Intellectual Property Association. "Copyright Industries in the U.S. Economy: 1977–1993." Washington, D.C., 1995.

National Science Board. "Science and Engineering Indicators, 1996." Washington, D.C.: National Science Foundation, 1996.

Bibliography

Nelson, Gary. "The Sufficiency of Copyright Protection in the Video Electronic Entertainment Industry: Comparing the US with the European Union." *Law and Policy in International Business* 27, no. 3, (1996, p. 805.

Nelson, Richard R., and Gavin Wright. "The Rise and Fall of American Technological Leadership: The Postwar Era in Historical Perspective." *Journal of Economic Literature,* vol. 30 (December 1992), pp. 1931–64.

Office of the U.S. Trade Representative. *The Uruguay Round: Growth for the World, Jobs for the US—A Primer* (December 1, 1993), p. 6.

Oksenberg, Michel, Pitman Potter, and William Abnett. "Advancing Intellectual Property Rights: Information Technologies and the Course of Economic Development in China." *NBR Analysis.* The National Bureau of Asian Research, vol. 7, no. 4 (November 1996).

Ostry, Sylvia. *Governments and Corporations in a Shrinking World.* New York: Council on Foreign Relations, 1990.

Primo Braga, Carlos Alberto. "The Newly Industrializing Economies." In *Global Dimensions of Intellectual Property Rights in Science and Technology.* Washington, D.C.: National Academy Press, 1993.

Primo Braga, Carlos Alberto. "Chile and NAFTA: The Services and Intellectual Property Rights Dimensions." Unpublished paper for the "Chile NAFTA Seminar" of the World Bank and the Ministry of Finance of Chile, Santiago, June 20, 1994.

Romer, Paul. "Two Strategies for Economic Development: Using Ideas and Producing Ideas." Proceedings of the World Bank Annual Conference on Development Economics, 1992. Washington, D.C.: the World Bank, 1993, pp. 63–91.

Schaffer, Jon. "Copyright Protected Industries Outpacing Other US Sectors." USIA, February 16, 1995. Visit their internet site at www.usia.gov/topics/ip/ipr58.

Schott, Jeffrey. *Uruguay Round: An Assessment.* Washington, D.C.: Institute for International Economics, 1994, pp. 115–23 and pp. 168–70.

Sell, Susan. "Intellectual Property Protection and Antitrust in the Developing World." *International Organization,* vol. 49, no. 2 (Spring 1995), pp. 315–49.

Sherwood, Robert M., and Carlos A. Primo Braga. "Intellectual Property, Trade and Economic Development: A Road Map for FTAA Negotiations." Unpublished paper, 1996.

Sherwood, Robert M. "Why a Uniform Intellectual Property System Makes Sense for the World." In *Global Dimensions of Intellectual Property Rights in Science and Technology.* Washington, D.C.: National Academy Press, 1993.

Software Publishers Association. *1995 Report on Global Software Piracy.* Washington, D.C., 1995.

Steinberg, Don. "Digital Underground." *Wired,* (January 1, 1997) pp. 104–110.

Steinberg, Richard. "The Uruguay Round: A Preliminary Analysis of the Final Act." In *Laws of International Trade.* February 1994.

Steinberg, Richard. "Transatlantic Management of the Global Trading System." In *Open for Business: Creating a Transatlantic Marketplace.* New York: Council on Foreign Relations, 1996, pp. 97–112.

Sykes, Alan O. "Constructive Unilateral Threats in International Commercial Relations: The Limited Case for Section 301." In *Law and Policy in International Business,* 23, no. 2 (1992), pp. 263–331.

TABD Progress Report. May 23, 1996. Internet site—http://iepnt1.-itaiep.doc.gov/ tabd/progress.

Thornton, Emily. "Some Like it Hot." *Far Eastern Economic Review,* (August 15, 1996) pp. 58-60.

Bibliography

Tyson, Laura D'Andrea. *Who's Bashing Whom?* Washington, D.C.: Institute for International Economics, 1992.

U.S. Bureau of the Census. "Statistical Abstract of the United States: 1995." (115th edition.) Washington, D.C., 1995, p. 398.

U.S. Constitution. Article 1, section 8 (1789).

U.S. Department of Commerce. *US Foreign Trade Highlights.* Washington, D.C., 1995, pp. 11–15.

US ITC. *Foreign Protection of Intellectual Property Rights and Its Effect on US Industry and Trade—Report to the US Trade Representative.* Investigation no. 332-245. Publication no. 2065. Washington, D.C., 1988.

USTR. "Fact Sheet: Chinese IPR Piracy Results in Fewer Jobs for US Workers." January 5, 1995.

USTR. "Fact Sheet: Intellectual Property Rights Enforcement in China." Unpublished, May 1996.

USTR. Fact Sheet: Special 301 on Intellectual Property Rights and 1996 Title VII Decisions. Internet site—http://www.ustr.gov/reports/special/ factsheets.htm.

USTR. "USTR Announces Two Decisions: Title VII and Special 301." Press release of April 30, 1996.

West, Joel. "Software Rights and Japan's Shift to an Information Society." *Asian Survey,* vol. 35, no. 12 (December 1995), pp. 1118–39.

World Bank. *Workers in an Integrating World.* New York: Oxford University Press, 1995, pp. 164–65.

Ye, Sang. "Computer Insect." *Wired* no. 4.7 (July 1996), p. 82.

Yu, Jianyang. "Protection of Intellectual Property in the PRC." *Pacific Basin Law Journal,* vol. 13, no. 140 (1994), pp. 140–62.